IAN H. JOHNSTONE
BRIDGEWATER STATE COLLEGE

ROBERT E. NYE
UNIVERSITY OF OREGON

E 70

LEARNING MUSIC WITH THE RECORDER

and other classroom instruments

PRENTICE-HALL, INC., Englewood Cliffs, New Jersey 07632

Library of Congress Cataloging in Publication Data

JOHNSTONE, IAN H (date)
 Learning music with the recorder and other classroom
instruments.

 Bibliography: p.
 Includes indexes.
 1. Music—Theory. 2. Recorder (Musical instrument)
—Methods. I. Nye, Robert Evans, joint author.
II. Title.
 MT6.J73L4   781   78-12203
 ISBN 0-13-527648-9

Printed in the United States of America

10 9 8 7 6 5 4 3 2 1

Editorial/production supervision by Ruth Anderson
Interior design by Fred Bernardi
Page layout by Gail Cocker
Cover design by Wanda Lubelska
Manufacturing Buyer: Phil Galea

PRENTICE-HALL INTERNATIONAL, INC., *London*
PRENTICE-HALL OF AUSTRALIA PTY. LIMITED, *Sydney*
PRENTICE-HALL OF CANADA, LTD., *Toronto*
PRENTICE-HALL OF INDIA PRIVATE LIMITED, *New Delhi*
PRENTICE-HALL OF JAPAN, INC., *Tokyo*
PRENTICE-HALL OF SOUTHEAST ASIA PTE. LTD., *Singapore*
WHITEHALL BOOKS LIMITED, *Wellington, New Zealand*

781
J73

CONTENTS

FOREWORD

Music educators have found that virtually all methods for recorder instruction are primarily concerned with recorder technique and performance; little material has been provided in them for learning music fundamentals and elements of methodology. *Learning Music with the Recorder and Other Classroom Instruments* was written to remedy this situation.

1. Music fundamentals are learned as the student performs musically.
2. The student becomes a performer of music on the recorder and other classroom instruments as well as vocally.
3. The student is introduced to elements of Orff and Kodàly procedures.
4. The book is written very simply so that children may begin using it in late third grade. Thus, the college students may "teach as they were taught" by using the book in their professional teaching.

The reader will find a step-by-step progression of musical experiences that assist the learner to form music concepts in logical sequence. Part 1 begins by providing experiences in rhythm, out of which melodic expression grows. Development of pitch perception begins with the descending minor third and progresses systematically and creatively through making music with the most commonly used pentatonic scales. Arnold Walter wrote: "Orff starts with the premise (learned from ethnomusicology) that musical development of children roughly corresponds to the growth of music in history: rhythm precedes (and is stronger than) melody; melody precedes (and is stronger than) harmony."*

*Arnold Walter, "Carl Orff's Music For Children," *The Instrumentalist*, XIII (January, 1959), pp. 38–39.

Speech patterns using words, phrases, or nursery rhymes are experienced first, then explained. These patterns are felt by stamping, clapping, and eventually through the use of instruments. Rhythm is also the first element used in teaching music by the great Hungarian composer-educator Zoltan Kodàly. After hearing and feeling the beat, the students begin to sense the beat from written notation.

From this rhythmic foundation melodies in the common pentatonic scales are played on the recorder and sung with tone syllables and the moveable *do*. The skills of hearing intervals and reading music are reinforced by employing Curwen hand signs. Kodàly believed that most young children cannot hear and sing the major diatonic scale in tune because the half steps are too difficult for them. Referring to the pentatonic scale *do re mi so la*, Kodàly stated that with those tones, a firm foundation can be built for beautiful singing and good understanding and love for noble music.

Part 2 encompasses other modes. Related rhythmic, melodic, and harmonic activities using classroom instruments and the voice are included throughout. The reader will find an abundance of songs and instrumental pieces along with experiences in improvisation, composition, and tonal memory games.

This approach to learning to play the recorder features beginning with the notes *A* and *C*, which provides a secure "hold" on the instrument with the left thumb and first and second fingers. Additional fingerings are learned in logical sequence as their relation to a pentatonic framework unfolds. Fingerings are drawn with a visual relationship between the held instrument and the printed page, which is more easily comprehended by the beginner. The book is written for the baroque (English) recorder because of its superior intonation and popularity.

The authors have endeavored to simplify and condense the content, keeping in mind the limited time available to most college classes. They solicit and accept with gratitude suggestions from users of this book that will further increase its capacity to satisfy their needs.

The authors acknowledge the numerous and specific suggestions of those who reviewed the manuscript.

I.H.J.

R.E.N.

(August, 1978)

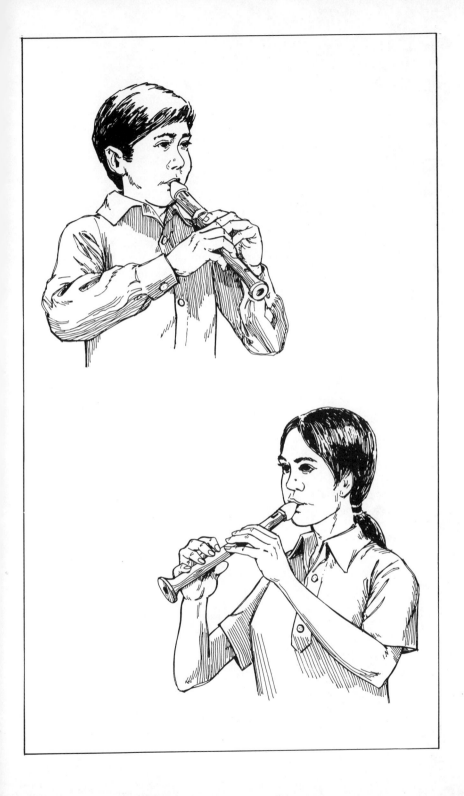

PART 1

PENTATONIC

UNIT 1

Exploring Sounds

Clap your hands.

How many ways can you clap your hands? Fast? Slow? Loud? Clap in ways to produce different sounds.

Stamp your feet in several ways to make different sounds.

Clap, then stamp the following stems in a variety of ways, such as slow, fast, soft, loud.

①

Clap and stamp at the same time for each stem.

Chant the following names: Bil-ly, Rob-ert, Har-ry, Su-sie, Ma-ry, Sal-ly.

Chant the names again, while you clap the stems.

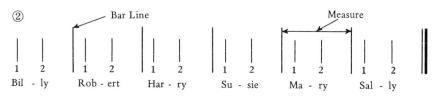

Clap the stems and say the numbers in example ②. Try to chant other names in your class as you clap the stems. Try it at different speeds. Use only names that fit your clapping; we will use other names later on.

The speed (fastness, slowness) at which we perform music is called *tempo*.

How many measures are in the next group of stems? Decide on a tempo first, clap it, then stamp it.

Clap, stamp, and chant the numbers at the same time.
Do the same for the next one. Remember to decide on a tempo first!

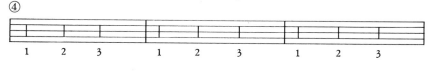

How does example ④ differ from example ③ ?
What is happening in ⑤ ?

Pick up your recorder with the fingers of your left hand, placing your left thumb as shown in the drawing.

Placement of the
left thumb

Explore sound with the recorder.

Place the instrument on your lower lip and close your mouth without touching the mouthpiece with your teeth.

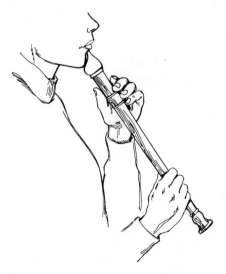

Preparatory position

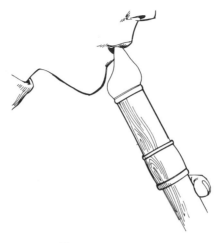

Placement of the mouth

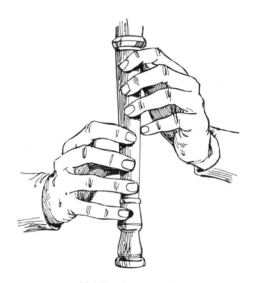

Holding the recorder

Blowing *very gently,* begin each tone by making a "dah" sound with your tongue. End each tone with a silent "t".

Here are some fingerings for making sounds.

• indicates that the hole is covered with the finger.

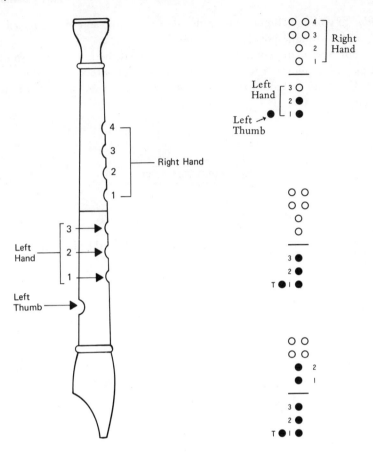

Make long and short tones using this fingering.

Sing *mi,* 3, or *A* to this pitch.

Play this sound repeatedly, counting *two* to yourself, *three* to yourself, or *four* to yourself. Remember to decide on a tempo and to begin each tone with a "dah" tongue position. Blow *gently*.

For how many counts (beats) can you hold this tone? How short can you play it? Remember to begin and end all tones with your tongue.

This tone is *A*, and the note is written on the second space from the bottom of the staff.

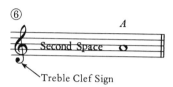

These five lines and the four spaces between the lines are called the *staff*.

Musical Notes

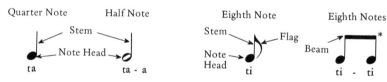

*Beam: flags joined together.

Instead of always counting numbers, we can say "ta" (pronounced tah) for each beat. Decide on a tempo, then clap and "ta" the beat. Now play this example on your recorder.

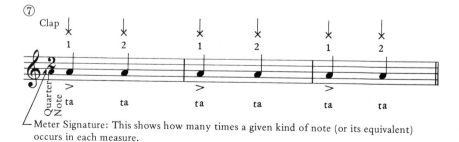

Meter Signature: This shows how many times a given kind of note (or its equivalent) occurs in each measure.

> Accent Mark (louder note): Apply the accent on the first beat of each measure.

Think the beat, play the starting note, and sing the following:

— The hand in this position is the sign for *mi* or *3*.

Think the beats, then clap, stamp, "ta", play, and sing *A* to this meter:

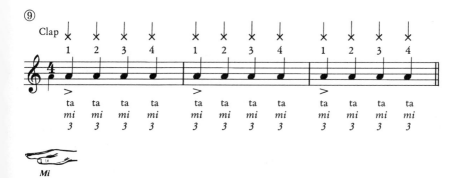

Look at the meter signature, then clap, stamp, "ta", play, and sing this one.

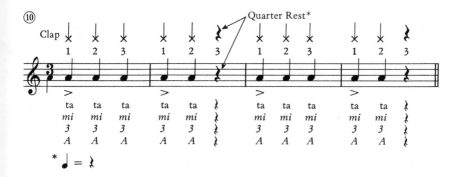

What is different here?

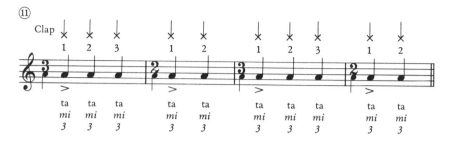

Clap, "ta", play, and sing this one. Remember to decide on a tempo and to begin each tone with "dah" and end it with an unpronounced "t".

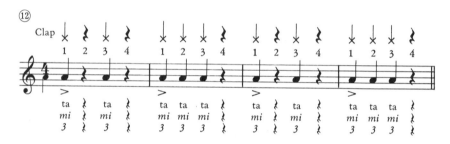

The preceding exercises have provided experiences with the beat (pulse). *Rhythm* is a grouping of sounds and silences of varying duration in relation to a regular beat.

Clap some beats or rhythms, and pick a classmate to play them using the note *A*. Examples:

This note is *C*. It is written on the third space from the bottom of the staff.

Play *C* on your recorder, and then play example ⑰. Remember to blow *gently* into the recorder.

Sing example ⑰

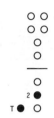

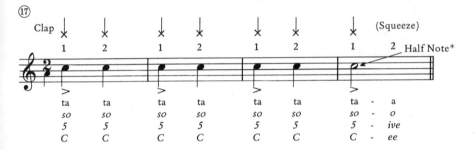

 — The hand in this position is the sign for *so* or *5*.

So

$$\ast \; \clubsuit = \clubsuit \; \clubsuit$$
ta - a   ta   ta

Two-Note Melodies

Play the two notes you have learned. Which one sounds higher in pitch?

Compose a four-measure tune using these two notes and write it in your book. Play or sing it for the class. Choose someone to play or sing your tune. Add words to make it a song if you wish.

Set a tempo, then clap, play, and sing this one.

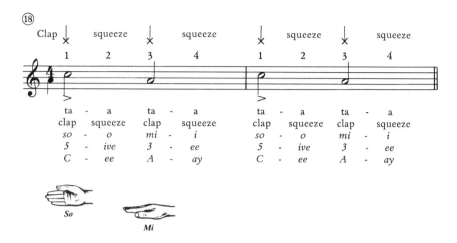

Do it again. This time stamp the beat; clap and "ta" the half notes. Stamping the beat indicates the four pulses per measure. Notice that each half note gets *two* stamps: ♩ = ♩ ♩ . Clapping the half notes indicates the rhythm of the melody.

Look at the meter signature, then sing these names.

Try to sing other names to these notes. Add Mark's name to the list.

Do you remember?

Stamp the beat, clap and "ta" the rhythm of the melody, and then play and sing the names.

Stamp the accent, clap the beat.

Question and Answer

Stamp the beat, clap the rhythm of the melody, and then play and sing the tunes with syllables and letter names.

First, stamp the beat. *Second,* clap and "ta" the rhythm of the words. *Third,* do all three together. *Fourth,* chant the words and clap the beat.

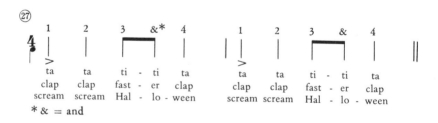

Stamp the beat and clap the rhythm of the melody. Play it, then sing it.

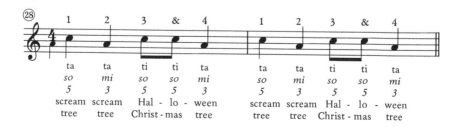

Using eighth and quarter notes, stamp the beat and clap the rhythm of the melody; then play and sing them.

The steady beat which is felt continuously throughout a musical composition is also called the *pulse*.

A *melody* is a succession of pitches. Melodies are often called tunes.

The *rhythm* of the melody in a song is usually the rhythm of the words.

Try creating your own music using eighth, quarter, and/or half notes.

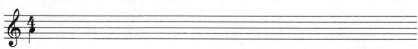

Two New Notes, G and *E*

Let's move *so* or 5 to the note *G* on the second line of the staff.

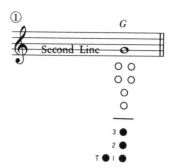

Think a tempo; then clap, play, and sing. Blow *gently*.

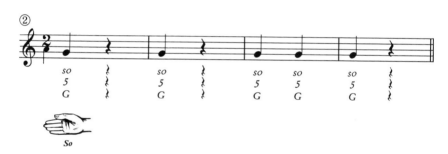

Using the *G* fingering, try to find the fingering for the new *mi* or 3 with your right hand. Listen very carefully for the *mi* sound.

The new *mi* or *3* fingering should look like this:

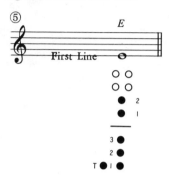

Play and sing this melody. Next, use the hand signs when you sing.

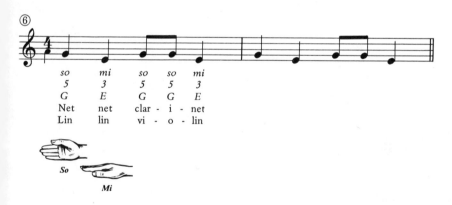

Music in More Than One Part
for Playing and Singing

Try this two-part song.

SANTA CLAUS

In the next song, how many beats are there in each measure? Stamp the beats, clap the rhythm of the melody, and chant the words. Now play it, then sing it.

Look at the song again. What kind of a note receives one beat?

$\frac{4}{4}$ means that there are four quarter notes ♩ or their *equivalent* in each measure.

RAIN, RAIN

Rain, Rain, go a - way,   come a - gain some oth - er day,

Clap

Stamp

Clap
Stamp

Lit - tle Sal - ly wants to play,   Rain, rain, go a - way.

Timbre

Try to think of some other rhythmic patterns in $\frac{4}{4}$. Try *Rain, Rain* using drum, triangle, tambourine, or other classroom instruments. What instrument would be the best to keep a *good, steady* beat? Divide the class into groups with one group playing the recorder while others sing and play the rhythmic patterns.

Play each instrument separately. Listen *very carefully* to the different kind of sound each instrument makes. How can you tell the sound of one instrument from another?

A stamp sounds different from a clap; a triangle sounds different from a drum; finger cymbals sound different from a tambourine because of their tone quality. Tone quality, tone color, or timbre (pronounced tăm-bur) is what we hear when we notice the differences in sound among different instruments or voices.

Classroom instruments may be grouped under the following headings. Group them in other ways, such as "low—high" "metal—wood— membrane—wind." Examples:

Nonpitched Percussion Instruments	*Pitched Percussion Instruments*
Rhythm Sticks	Resonator Bells
Jingle Bells	Xylophone
Tambourine	Step Bells
Tone Block	
Triangle	*Recorder-type Instruments*
Sand Blocks	
Drum	
Finger Cymbals	Song Flute
Cymbals	Tonette
Temple Blocks	Flutophone
Castanets	Recorder
Claves	
Maracas	*Autoharp*
Guiro	
Gong	
Bongo Drums	
Conga Drum	

Compose a piece of music using recorder and classroom instruments. Here is a beginning. Complete it.

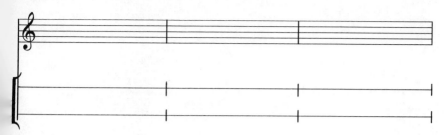

Another *Rain, Rain*:

RAIN, RAIN

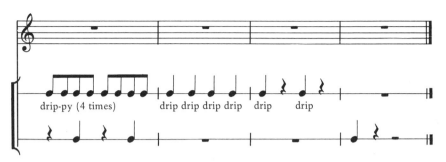

Do you remember the name and the fingering for this note? This time we will call it *la* or *6*.

— The hand in this position is the sign for *la* or *6*.

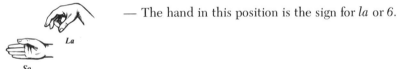

You now know hand signs for three pitches, *so*, *mi*, and *la*, or *5*, *3*, and *6*.

Make up a game in which the leader makes hand signs and the class sings or plays what the hand tells them to do.

JACK AND JILL

Provide an accompaniment for this song by completing the percussion instrument and drum parts of the score.

LITTLE DROPS OF WATER

22

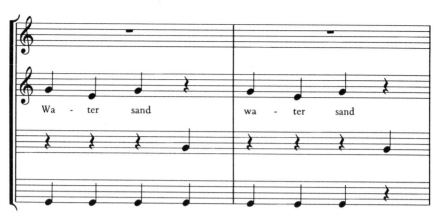

make the might - y   o - cean   and the plea - sant land.

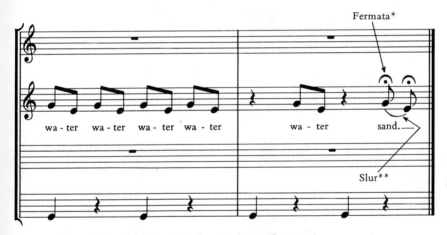

Fermata*

wa - ter   wa - ter   wa - ter   wa - ter   wa - ter   sand.

Slur**

Fermata: pause; that is, hold the note longer than usual.
**Slur:* connect notes of different pitch without tonguing them.

UNIT 3

Intervals

ta   ta   ta   ta   ta - a ta - a   ta   ta   ta   ta   ta - a ta - a
so   so   mi   la   so   mi   so   so   mi   la   so   mi
5   5   3   6   5   3   5   5   3   6   5   3
Ring a - round the ros - ies,   poc - ket full of pos - ies!

An interval is the difference in pitch between two tones sounded in succession.

To find and name any interval, always call the note you are beginning with "1", and count up or down the lines and spaces to the other note. For example, the notes A and G in example ③ form the interval of a *second* because one counts from 1 to 2.

The interval from G to E is a *third*.

The interval from E to A is a *fourth*.

Find the intervals in the song *Ring Around the Rosies*.

Name these intervals:

Octave

What intervals are in this song?

MERRY CHRISTMAS

We wish you mer - ry, mer - ry, mer - ry Christ - mas,

Christ-mas cheer loud and clear for the best time of the year.

Let's sing and play *Merry Christmas* again, adding melody, bells and drum.

Recorder & Singing

Mallet Instruments
Hold a mallet in each hand

Drum

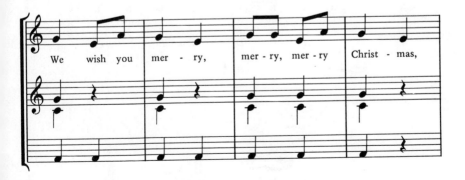

We wish you mer - ry, mer - ry, mer - ry Christ - mas,

Christ - mas, cheer | loud and clear | for the best time | of the year.

Two New Notes, *D* and *C*

ta	ta	ta	ta		ta	ta	ta	-	ta
mi	re	do	re		mi	mi	mi	-	i
3	2	1	2		3	3	3	-	ee
E	D	C	D		E	E	E	-	ee

Mi

Re

Do

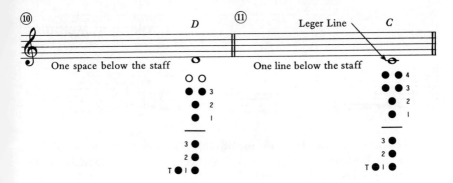

Blow *very gently* when playing this low *C*. Make sure all the holes are covered.

Try this melody. Can you name it?

*Whole note = 4 beats.

HOT CROSS BUNS

Traditional Song

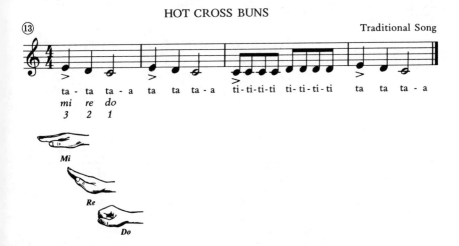

The arrow shows that the melody moves from one note to another *without* any lines or spaces in between. We say the melody moves by *step*. How does this melody move?

Because there are lines or spaces in between the notes of this melody, we say the melody moves by *skip*. Listen to this melody on a recording of Haydn's "Surprise" Symphony, second movement.

Does this melody move by step, skip, or both?

AU CLAIR DE LA LUNE
(In The Evening Moonlight)

French Folk Tune

As you sing and listen to *Au Clair de la Lune,* you will sense that the tune moves forward to the end of the word "Pierrot," where it seems to come to a pause, and that then it progresses until it reaches the word "note". Such pauses in music mark the end of a musical *phrase*. A phrase might be compared to a sentence in speech or in writing. A phrase expresses a complete musical thought. How many phrases are there in this melody? Do they sound the same, or do they sound different?

To hear phrases that sound the same or phrases that sound different means you have sensed the *form* in the music. *Unity* and *variety* make *form;* unity can be represented by repetition of like or near-like phrases; variety can be supplied by contrasting phrases.

Look again at the notes of this melody.

Let's listen to tones *C, E,* and *G* played or sung together by three people, or three groups.

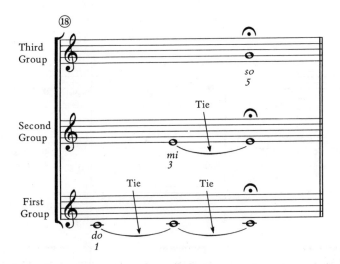

Do you like the sound? Describe it to the class. Find it on the piano, bells, and Autoharp and play it. You have just played or sung the *C major chord. A chord* is a combination of three or more tones sounding together. Chords produce *harmony* when they change from one to another.

A *tie* is a curved line (⌣) connecting two or more notes of the *same pitch;* it unites them into a single sound.

Where have you heard this tune before? What is different about it this time?

Again,

HOT CROSS BUNS

One a pen - ny, Two a pen - ny | Hot Cross Buns!

mi   re   do

Pentatonic Scale

Play and sing the following notes, and listen very carefully to their sound. Blow very gently.

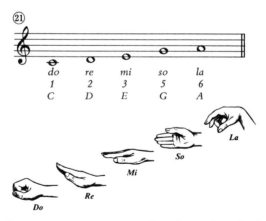

(21)

do   re   mi   so   la
1   2   3   5   6
C   D   E   G   A

This is a five-tone or *pentatonic* scale. This scale is built on C. C is *do* or *1*. You now know the hand signs for a pentatonic scale. Play the game in which the leader makes hand signs and the class sings or plays what the hand tells them to do.

We can rearrange this scale to begin on different notes. Listen to the sound as you play (a) and (b) on your recorder. Play (c), (d), and (e) on the bells or the piano. Try to sing these pentatonic scales.

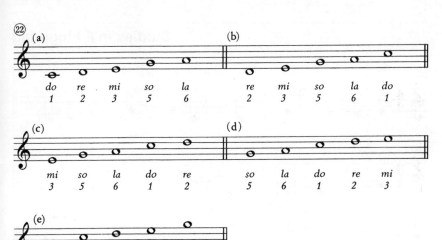

There are many songs which use a pentatonic scale. Play and sing this one.

WHO'S THAT TAPPING AT THE WINDOW?

American Folk Song

| ta - a ta - a | ti - ti | ti - ti ta | ta | ta - a ta - a | ti - ti | ti - ti ta |

| do | so | re | re | mi | mi | re | do |
| 1 | 5 | 2 | 2 | 3 | 3 | 2 | 1 |

Who's that tap-ping at the win-dow? Who's that knock-ing at the door?
Bil - ly's* tap-ping at the win-dow. Mar - y's knock-ing at the door.

*Use names of children in the class.

Play and listen to the melody again. You will notice that the melody seems to center around the tone *C*. This tonal center is called the *home tone* or *tonic*. The last note of a song is almost always the tonic.

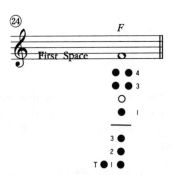

Name and finger all the notes of this song.

Of course you remember the song! It is in a pentatonic scale built on *F*. *F* is *do* or *1*. What is the tonic of this scale?

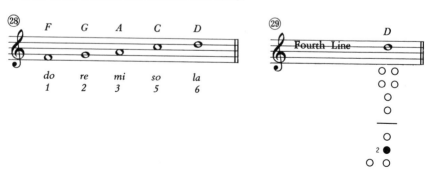

What other *D* have you learned? Play one then the other. Do they sound the same? Is one a higher sound than the other? Do the same with the tone *C*. This distance between low *D* and high *D* and between low *C* and high *C* is called an *octave*.

This pentatonic song may be one of your favorites. Play it, sing it! What is its tonic?

OLD MACDONALD

Find the *F* chord on Autoharp, piano, and mallet instruments. Improvise an accompaniment to *Old MacDonald* while others sing or play the recorder.

Examine the last measure of *Old MacDonald*.

A dotted half note (𝅗𝅥.) gets *three* beats or pulses, because a dot adds one-half the value of the note that it follows.

𝅗𝅥.   =   ♩ ♩ ♩   =   three quarter notes tied together

            ta - a - a   to make a longer sound.

UNIT 4

New Notes for the Recorder

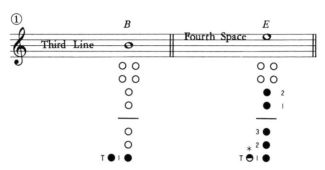

* ◐ means thumb hole slightly open.

Compare the sounds of the two notes. Watch the thumb fingering!
Octave drill on *E:*

Play example ③ while you listen carefully to each note. Sing it. What is the name of this kind of scale?

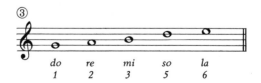

36

Ostinato and Bourdon

In what pentatonic scale do you think *Old MacDonald* is written this time? What is its tonic?

Cowbell Trill

Compare the *ostinato* and *bourdon* in this piece. Compose an ostinato of your own and experiment by playing it with *Old MacDonald.*

Melodic Patterns

Let's play a memory game! Listen, then sing and play the following melodic patterns after your teacher plays them on the recorder. Sing each melody to syllables or numbers before you play it. All melodies are in the pentatonic scale of *F*. First, play and sing the scale beginning on the lowest note, then on the highest note.

Before the teacher plays each complete melody, you may wish to hear the *first* note of each pattern and to be told its syllable name or number. Now close your book and *listen* in order to be ready to sing and play what you hear.

Make up some melodic patterns with your recorder. Use them to play the memory game, but this time *you* are the teacher. Think the sound of the tonic firmly in your mind.

Try a question-and-answer pattern. The first player will play or sing a musical question; the second player will play or sing an answer.

Examples:

Using the pentatonic scales on *C*, *F*, or *G*, compose and play melodies for the sayings in numbers ④⓪ and ④①. Write them on the staves provided.

Examples:

do   so   Cold   as   ice!

Slip - per - y   as   an   eel!
tri - o - la   ti - ti   ta

do   so   Pig   pig   guin - ea   pig!

do   so   Fred - die   where   are   you?

* A triplet is a group of three notes performed in the place of two of the same kind. It is indicated by a *3* placed over or under the notes.

Snug   as   a   bug   in   a   rug

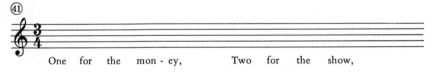

One   for   the   mon - ey,   Two   for   the   show,

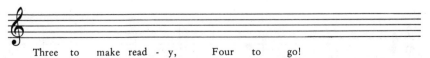

Three   to   make   read - y,   Four   to   go!

Finish *Old Mother Witch* in C pentatonic. Eighth notes will be useful.

Old   Moth - er   Witch!   Fell   in   a   ditch!

Picked   up   a   pen - ny   and   thought   she   was   rich!

Other Pentatonic Scales

Some pentatonic scales can be played on the black keys of the piano and bells. Play this one first on the black keys, then on the white keys.

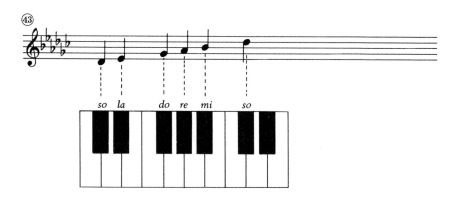

so   la   do   re   mi   so

Play and sing this Canadian folk song.

LAND OF THE SILVER BIRCH

D minor   Canadian Folk Song

la   mi   la
Land   of   the   sil - ver   birch,   home   of   the

What is the home tone or tonic of this tune?
This melody is in a pentatonic scale built on *D*.

Try imitating Indian drums on the piano by adding the following *bourdon* to *Land of the Silver Birch*. Play the bourdon on the piano or metallophone (whichever you think sounds the best). What interval is this bourdon?

Repeat Sign

You can change the bourdon. For example, the two notes could be played one after the other, and other notes within the pentatonic scale could be added.

TROT, PONY, TROT

E minor (21-chord Autoharp)   Chinese Folk Song

mi   la   mi   so   la   so   mi
3   6   3   5   6   5   3
Trot, trot   pon - y trot!   Trot to Grand-ma's gate - way.

so   mi so   la   la mi   so   mi so   la
She'll come out and call her dog, And then we'll ride on jog - a - jog,

Trot,   trot   pon - y trot!   Trot,   trot   pon - y   trot!

This melody is written in a pentatonic scale built on *E*.

E   G   A   B   D   E
la   do   re   mi   so   la

The following patterns could be used also as an introduction or coda (ending section) to the song.

What intervals are these accompanying patterns?

Bells or
Alto Metallophone

Bells or
Other Mallet
Instruments

Bells

Temple
Blocks

UNIT 5

Review of Note Values

Step the beat and clap the rhythm of the melody. Sing it, then play it.

THE BIG CLOCK

① F   Traditional Song

ta   ta - a
do   mi
Slow - ly ticks the big clock: tick - tock,

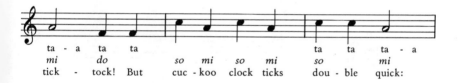

ta - a ta   ta   ta   ta   ta - a
mi   do   so mi so mi   so   mi
tick - tock! But cuc - koo clock ticks dou - ble quick:

ti ti ti ti   ti ti ti ti ti
do re mi re   do mi so mi do
Tick - a - tock - a, tick - a - tock - a, tick - a - tock - a, tick!

Read the meter signature in example ②. Do the note values affect the tempo?

Again,

THE BIG CLOCK

② C

ti   ti   ta   ta
do   mi   do
Slow - ly ticks the big clock: tick - tock,

ta   ti - ti   ti - ti   ti ti ta
mi   do   so mi   so so mi
tick - tock! But cuc - koo clock ticks dou - ble quick:

ti - ri - ti - ri ti - ri - ti - ri ti - ri - ti - ri ti
do re mi re   do mi so mi do
tick - a - tock - a, tick - a - tock - a, tick - a - tock - a, tick!

Sixteenth Note   ta = ti - ti = ti - ri - ti - ri

Check the meter signature, think a tempo, step the beat, then clap the rhythm of the notes:

BIG CLOCK, ALARM CLOCK, CUCKOO CLOCK

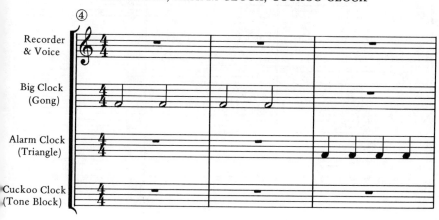

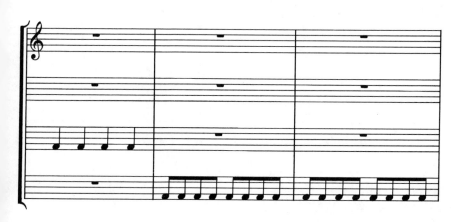

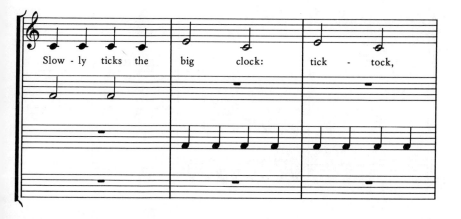

Slow - ly ticks the   big   clock: tick - tock,

tick - tock! But   cuc - koo clock ticks   dou - ble   quick:

tick- a-tock - a, tick - a - tock - a,   tick - a - tock-a,   tick!

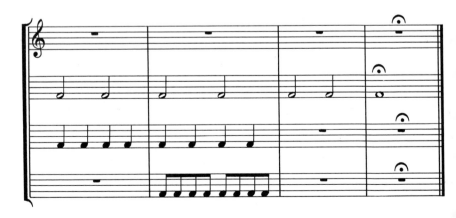

Pentatonic Songs to Sing and Play

The following pentatonic songs can be developed creatively, beginning with bourdon and ostinato as exemplified in *Old MacDonald,* pages 37–38. These can be altered, added to, and expanded in experimental ways; percussion sounds and movement may be added. The music can be taped and played for the students to help them hear and evaluate what they have done and decide whether their performance is acceptable or if they wish to make changes.

SCOTLAND'S BURNING

Scot-land's burn-ing, Scot-land's burn-ing, Fetch the wa-ter, Fetch the wa-ter,

Fire! fire! fire! fire! Pour on wa-ter, Pour on wa-ter.

CHATTER WITH THE ANGELS

Chat-ter with the an-gels soon in the morn-ing,

Chat-ter with the an-gels in that land.

Chat-ter with the an-gels soon in the morn-ing,

Chat-ter with the an-gels join that band!

⑦

I'M GONNA SING

Spiritual

I'm gon - na sing when the spir - it says "Sing,"

Eighth Rest

I'm gon - na sing when the spir - it says "Sing,"____

I'm gon - na sing when the spir - it says "Sing,"

And o - bey the spir - it of the Lord.

* An explanation of the upbeat or anacrusis will be found on page 78.

GOOD-BYE, OL' PAINT

⑧ **Smoothly**

Cowboy Song

My foot in the stir - rup, my pon - y won't stan';____

I'm a - leav - in' Chey - enne an' I'm off for Mon - tan'.____

Good - bye, ol' Paint, I'm a - leav - in' Chey - enne.

*An explanation of the dotted quarter note will be found on page 76.

2. I'm riding ol' Paint and a-leading ol' Fan;
Goodbye, little Annie, I'm off to Montan'.

3. Go hitch up your horses and give them some hay,
And seat yourself by me as long as you stay.

LI'L 'LIZA JANE

⑨ **Gaily**   American Folk Song

I got a house in Bal - ti - more, Li'l 'Li - za Jane,

Street cars run right by my door, Li'l 'Li - za Jane.

Oh! E - li - za, Li'l 'Li - za Jane;

Oh! E - li - za, Li'l 'Li - za Jane.

* **2/2** meter indicates that there are two beats in each measure and that a half-note or its equivalent receives one beat.

2. *I got a house in Baltimore, Li'l 'Liza Jane,*
Brussels carpet on my floor, Li'l 'Liza Jane,

3. *I got a house in Baltimore, Li'l 'Liza Jane,*
Silver doorplate on my door, Li'l 'Liza Jane.

4. *Come, my love, and marry me, Li'l 'Liza Jane,*
And I'll take good care of thee, Li'l 'Liza Jane.

GRANDMA GRUNTS

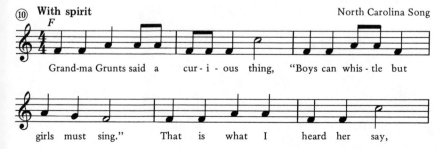

⑩ **With spirit**   North Carolina Song

Grand-ma Grunts said a cur - i - ous thing, "Boys can whis - tle but

girls must sing." That is what I heard her say,

'Twas no long-er than yes-ter-day. Boys can whis-tle,

(whistle)   Girls must sing, tra la la la la!

2. *Boys can whistle, of course they may,*
They can whistle the livelong day.
Why can't girls whistle too, pray tell,
If they manage to do it well?

3. *Grandma Grunts said it wouldn't do,*
Gave a very good reason too:
Whistling girls and crowing hens
Always come to some bad ends.

MARY HAD A BABY

Spiritual

Ma-ry had a ba-by, yes, Lord,

Ma-ry had a ba-by, yes, my Lord,

Ma-ry had a ba-by, yes, Lord, The

peo-ple keep a-com-in' but the train done gone.

2. *Laid Him in a manger.*

3. *Shepherds came to see Him.*

4. *Angels sang His glory.*

I'VE BEEN TO HAARLEM

Sea Chantey

I've been to Haar - lem, I've been to Do - ver,

I've trav - eled this wide world all o - ver,

O - ver, o - ver, three times o - ver, Find me an - o-ther ship

when this trip is o - ver. Sail - ing east, sail - ing west,

Sail - ing o - ver the o - cean, Bet-ter watch out when the

boat be - gins to rock or you'll lose your girl in the o - cean.

GO, TELL IT ON THE MOUNTAIN

Spiritual

When I was a seek - er, I sought both night and day,

I asked the Lord to help me, And He showed me the

way.   Go   tell it on the moun - tain,

O - ver the hills and   eve - ry - where,___   Go   tell it on the

moun - tain, That   Je - sus Christ___ is   born.

THE FOUNTAIN

French Canadian Song

One   night as   I   lay dream - ing,   Lost   in   a

rev - er - ie,   I   heard   a   love - ly   foun - tain,

Play - ing   so   close   to   me;   Some - where that

foun - tain is flow - ing,   I   won - der, where can it be?

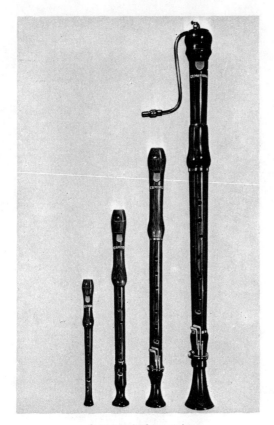

A consort of recorders

Soprano, alto, tenor, and bass recorders. Photograph courtesy of Trophy Music Company, 1278 W. 9th St., Cleveland, Ohio 44113.

PART 2

DIATONIC

UNIT 6

Adding *Fa* or *4*

Compare the following scales:

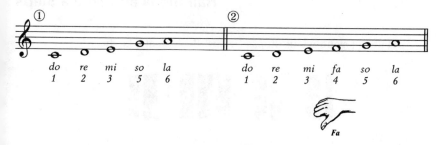

Play them on your recorder, then sing them. What has been added in number ②? Let's play, then sing *so, fa, mi* (*5, 4, 3*), beginning on different notes.

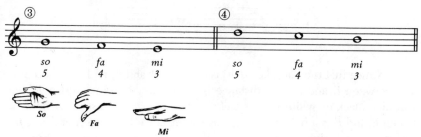

57

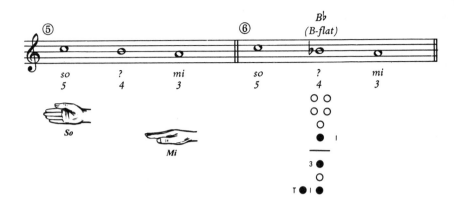

Play ⑤ and ⑥ again. Which one has the *so, fa, mi* sound? Which note makes the difference? How? Can you explain what a *flat* (♭) does to a note?

A *flat* (♭) lowers the pitch of a note one half step. If you are not sure, listen to the sound of *B* and *B* ♭ again.

Half Steps and Whole Steps

Half steps and whole steps can best be seen at a keyboard.

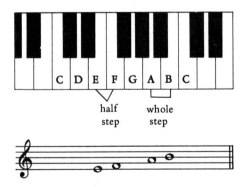

Notice that the black key (*B* ♭) is between *A* and *B*, and that there is *no* key between *E* and *F*. The distance from one key to its nearest neighbor, whether black or white key, is called a *half step*. The distance, then, between *E* and *F* is a half step, whereas the distance between *A* and *B* is *two* half steps, or a whole step.

Play these two intervals on the piano, bells, or recorder and listen to the difference in sound between them. Compare the half steps between *E* and *F* and between *A* and *B*♭.

Play and sing the following melodies with the correct syllables or numbers, whether they are written under the notes or not. Try singing them with letter names, too.

Key Signature: one flat. Notice that the flat sign is on the *B* line, the third line from the bottom. This means that every *B* throughout the piece is played as *B-flat* and *not* as *B-natural* (♮). A piece in major tonality that has one flat (*B*♭) as its key signature is in the key of *F*. That means its home tone or tonic is *F*.

VIVA LA MUSICA

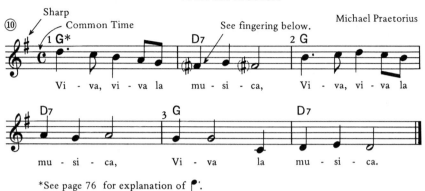

Vi - va, vi - va la mu - si - ca,   Vi - va, vi - va la

mu - si - ca,   Vi - va   la   mu - si - ca.

*See page 76 for explanation of ♩͑.

Piano Chording:

"C" is the first letter of the word "common." Common time (meter) signature is another way of writing $\frac{4}{4}$.

If a flat (♭) indicates that a note sounds one *half step lower* in pitch, what do you think a *sharp* (♯) does to a note?

Compare and discuss the sound of these pairs of notes. After playing them on the recorder, relate them to the piano keyboard.

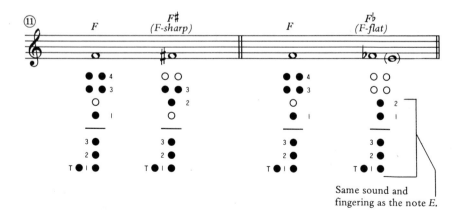

Same sound and fingering as the note E.

A piece in major tonality that has one sharp ($\sharp$) as its key signature is in the key of G. A piece with a key signature of one flat ($\flat$) is in what key? When there are no sharps or flats in the key signature, we are usually in the key of C.

Learn the rhythm first; then play, sing, and enjoy this folk song.

FOUR IN A BOAT

Appalachian Folk Song

Four in a boat and the tide rolls high,

Four in a boat and the tide rolls high,

Four in a boat and the tide rolls high,

Wait-ing for a pret-ty one to come bye and bye.

*B=II: Alternate fingering, discussed below.

Piano:

Use the Autoharp and some nonpitched classroom instruments to add variety to the song.

Autoharp*

Photograph courtesy of Oscar Schmidt-International, Inc., and Music Education Group, Union, New Jersey 07083.

B-II stands for a substitute or alternate fingering. Here are the two fingerings for *B*.

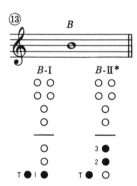

*A book that takes the Autoharp player from the first steps to skilled player levels and explains how the instrument is employed in teaching music is *Teaching Music With the Autoharp,* by Robert Nye and Meg Peterson, published by Music Education Group, Box 1501, Union, New Jersey 07083.

It is easier to *add* a finger than to *change* fingers.

Musical Form

German Folk Tune

*Breathe only at breath marks (𝄾).

How many measures of music are in this *German Folk Tune?* Measures group themselves into phrases forming a musical idea, a contrasting idea, or a repeated idea. (Hint: In *German Folk Tune*, consider the first four measures as a phrase, and call it "A"; or you might wish to draw a picture of it, such as ☐). We are trying to sense the form of the music. To do this, we try to hear phrases that sound the same, and phrases that sound different. It is this *unity* and *variety* which make form.

A B A Form (sometimes A A B A), as in *German Folk Tune.*

> A = first musical idea
> B = second (contrasting) musical idea
> A = first musical idea repeated

This design is known as A B A (☐○☐) form, *three-part* form, or *ternary* form.

A B Form

> A = first musical idea
> B = second (contrasting) musical idea

This design is *binary* or *two-part* form.

Unitary Form

> A = first musical idea
> A = repetition of first musical idea

This design is called *unitary* or one-idea form.

WHISTLE, DAUGHTER, WHISTLE

American Folk Song

What is the form of this song? There are no sharps or flats, which means that the piece is written in what key? Find *do* or *1* and decide which syllable or number the melody begins on.

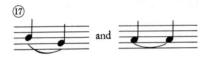

In the second measure we have "whis-tle, and." This rhythm is the result of an accent (>) on the second beat, rather than on the first beat, where it normally occurs. This situation of a shifted accent is called *syncopation*. (See *Li'l 'Liza Jane* in Unit 5 and *Cindy* in Unit 10 for other examples of syncopation.)

Slur and Tie

In *German Folk Tune* we made use of the slur. A curved line represents a *slur* and a *tie*. Can you remember the difference between the two? If not, look back on pages 23 and 30. In playing a slur on the recorder, you tongue only the first note.

Try completing this tune or composing a song, using either your own design or a design in unitary, binary, or ternary form. Be able to explain the phrases you use. Are they the same, different, or almost the same as other phrases in your piece? Use phrases of two, three, or four measures.

Tunes to Look at and to Play

In what key is number ⑲ written? Do the melody and harmony parts begin on the same note? Do they end on the same note? After you find *do* or *1,* sing the song to syllables or numbers. When you play it, think about the slurs and the substitute fingering for *B.*

Duet
⑲   German Folk Song

GO TELL AUNT RHODY

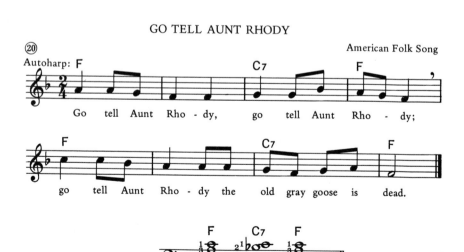

⑳   American Folk Song

Go tell Aunt Rho - dy, go tell Aunt Rho - dy;

go tell Aunt Rho - dy the old gray goose is dead.

66

In what key is *Go Tell Aunt Rhody* written? Does the song begin with the tonic note? Does the song end with the tonic note? If we call the first-line phrase "A", what could we call the second line? Then what is the form of the song?

JINGLE BELLS

J. Pierpont

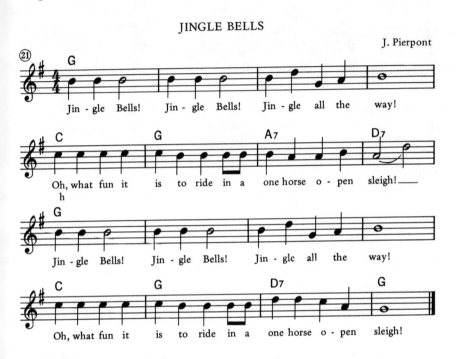

Jingle Bells has repeated and contrasting phrases. Explain the form to the class. Improvise a rhythmic accompaniment to the song, using nonpitched classroom instruments. Try playing the song, first using the regular fingering for *B*, then the alternate fingering. Which do you think is better? Why?

LIGHTLY ROW

German Folk Song

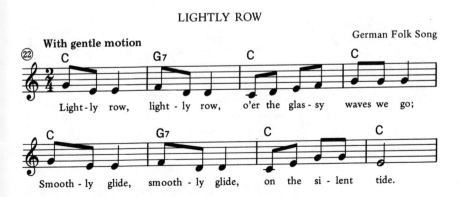

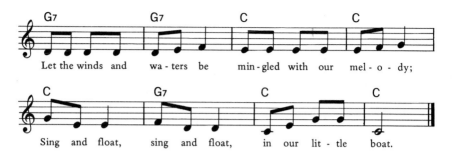

Let the winds and wa - ters be min - gled with our mel - o - dy;

Sing and float, sing and float, in our lit - tle boat.

In songs, the musical phrases often correspond to the lines of the text. How many phrases are there in *Lightly Row?* What do you think the form is? The syllable names or numbers can be sung easily with the tune.

Songs begin on other notes besides *do* or *1*. *Mi (3)* and *so (5)* are often used to begin songs.

Here is a list of well-known songs; try to play them on your recorder.

		First Notes:
1.	*When the Saints Go Marching In*	C, F, or G
2.	*This Old Man*	G, C, or D
3.	*Baa, Baa, Black Sheep*	C, F, or G
4.	*London Bridge*	G, C, or D
5.	*Hickory, Dickory, Dock*	E, A, or B
6.	*It's a Small World*	F

MY LITTLE DUCKLINGS

Austrian Folk Song

All my lit - tle duck - lings, Swim-ming here and there,

Heads are in the wa - ter, Tails are in the air.

All my little ducklings
Swimming round and round,
Now they're right side up
And now they're upside down.

Piano:
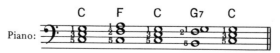

The lines of the text suggest phrases in this song. Where do you think the first phrase begins and ends?* Are there any skips in the melody? Find and play a scale-like passage. Find a repeated-note pattern.

UNIT 7

Moving Upward

If you don't remember the fingering for F ♯ , refer to page 60, number ⑪.

Key Signature: one sharp. Notice that the sharp sign is on the *F* line, the fifth line from the bottom of the staff. This means every *F* throughout the

*Children often find two-measure phrases, whereas some adults find four-measure phrases. Both are acceptable.

piece is played as *F-sharp* and *not F-natural* (♮). The above example, which
has one sharp (F♯) as its key signature, is in the key of *G*. *G* is its home tone
or tonic.

Diatonic Major Scales

Diatonic refers to scales having eight tones to an octave, such as the regular tones of major keys or minor keys (see p. 73).

The Major Scale

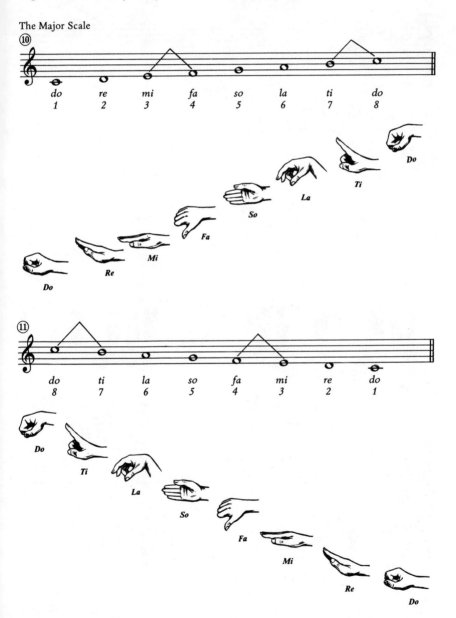

⑩

do	re	mi	fa	so	la	ti	do
1	2	3	4	5	6	7	8

Do · Re · Mi · Fa · So · La · Ti · Do

⑪

do	ti	la	so	fa	mi	re	do
8	7	6	5	4	3	2	1

Do · Ti · La · So · Fa · Mi · Re · Do

Play the hand-sign game again. Now the leader can use all the signs of the major scale, and the class will sing or play what the hand tells them to do.

Relating primary chords to the scale:

Primary chords in root position

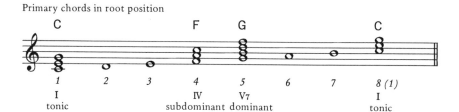

Relating notation to the keyboard:

The Grand Staff

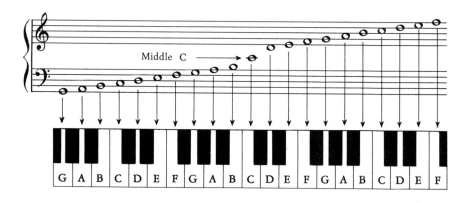

The C major scale, using different rhythms:

JOY TO THE WORLD

Isaac Watts

George F. Handel
Arr. by Lowell Mason

Joyously

Joy to the world! The Lord is come; Let earth re - ceive her King; _____ Let ev - 'ry _____ heart _____ pre - pare _____ Him _____ room, _____ And heav'n and na - ture _____ sing, And _____ heav'n and na - ture _____ sing, And _____ heav'n _____ and heav'n _____ and na - ture sing.

Play the C major scale on a keyboard and find where the half steps occur.

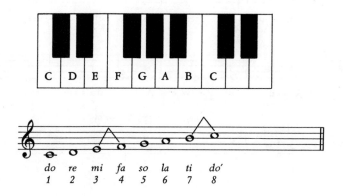

do re mi fa so la ti do'
1 2 3 4 5 6 7 8

Looking at a keyboard, write major scales on *F* and *G*. Remember where the half steps are placed. Use a flat or sharp where necessary, placing it to the left of the note.

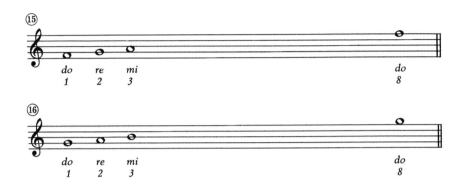

₍₁₅₎

    do   re   mi   do
    1   2   3   8

₍₁₆₎

    do   re   mi   do
    1   2   3   8

Unison and Harmony

IN THE EVENING MOONLIGHT

Andante (tempo marking: means "slowly")   French Folk Tune

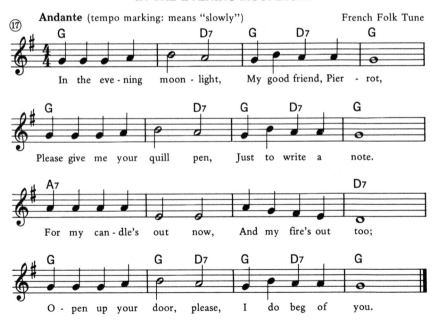

In the eve-ning moon-light, My good friend, Pier - rot,

Please give me your quill pen, Just to write a note.

For my can-dle's out now, And my fire's out too;

O - pen up your door, please, I do beg of you.

The above song has a definite form. The phrases tell you what it is. In what key is the song written?

IN THE EVENING MOONLIGHT

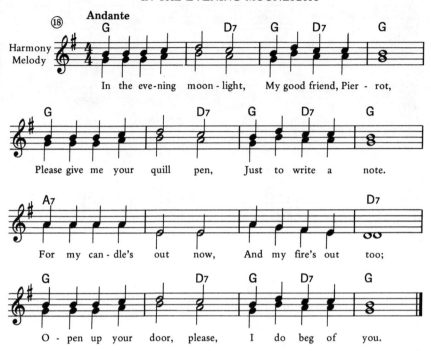

Compare music performed in *unison* with music performed in *harmony*. Which do you like better? Why? At what interval is the harmony part written? After practicing this song in $\frac{4}{4}$ meter, try performing it in $\frac{2}{2}$ meter, in which a half note receives one beat. An explanation of this meter is given o page 82.

Dotted Notes

AMERICA

Samuel Francis Smith   Henry Carey

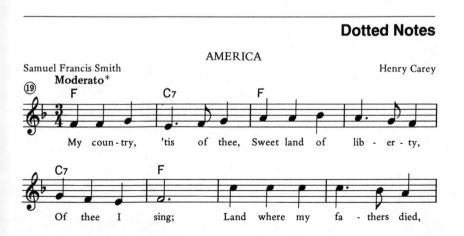

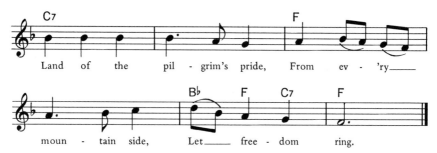

Land of the pil - grim's pride, From ev - 'ry____
moun - tain side, Let____ free - dom ring.

*Definitions of common musical terms are in Appendix G.

Piano:

Stamp the beat and clap the following rhythmic patterns.

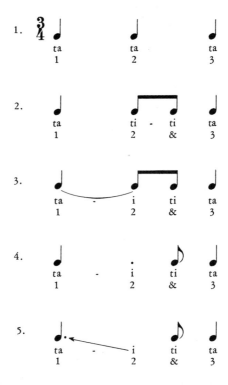

Remember, a dot placed after a note adds one-half the value of the note that it follows.

$$\text{𝅗𝅥. = 𝅗𝅥 ♩} \qquad \text{♩. = ♩ ♪} \qquad \text{♪. = ♪ 𝅘𝅥𝅯}$$

ta - a - a   ta - i   ti - m

How many beats (pulses) does the last note (𝅗𝅥.) of *America* receive?

Looking at the Music

ODE TO JOY

Ludwig Van Beethoven

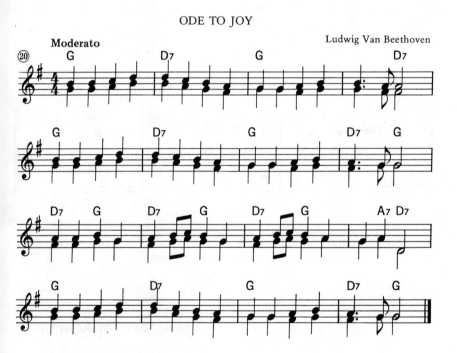

Moderato

The tune to *Ode to Joy* is from the last movement of Beethoven's Ninth Symphony. What are the syllables or numbers for the melody? Does the melody move mostly by step or by skip? In what form is the music? You can hear this melody played and sung on a recording of the last movement of Beethoven's Ninth Symphony.

A CRADLE HYMN

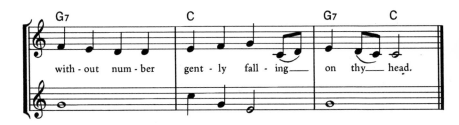

Are the phrases in this song the same, nearly the same, or different? Sing *do* or *1,* and then sing the first note of the melody.

The Upbeat or Anacrusis

So far, almost all the music we have played has started on the first beat of the measure. Many songs, however, begin on other pulses, usually on the last beat of the measure. Such songs are said to begin with an *upbeat* or *anacrusis.* The next song begins on the last pulse, which is the third beat in $\frac{3}{4}$ time. In order to complete a full measure of three pulses, the other two beats are found at the end of the piece.

Rule to Remember: Whenever a piece has an upbeat, the beats necessary to complete the upbeat's measure are found at the end of the composition.

WE WISH YOU A MERRY CHRISTMAS

English Carol

This song is in the key of *G*. The first note of the piece begins on *so* or 5 *below* the tonic.

LITTLE SANDMAN

Johannes Brahms

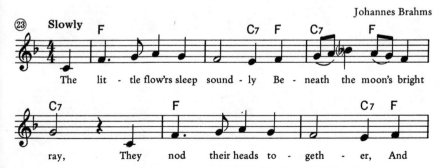

dream — the night — a - way.　　The — bud - ding trees wave
to　　and fro, And — mur - mur soft and low. ———
Sleep — on,　　sleep — on, — sleep — on, my — lit - tle one!

Study the words of *Little Sandman* and decide whether they should be sung softly or loudly. The degree of softness or loudness in music is called *dynamics.** After deciding which phrases are alike and which are different, outline the form on the chalkboard.

ALL THROUGH THE NIGHT

Traditional Welsh Lullaby

Moderato

Sleep, my child, and peace at - tend thee, All　through the　night;
Guard - ian an - gels God will send thee, All　through the　night.
Soft the drow- sy　hours are creep-ing, Hill and vale in　slum - ber steep-ing,
I　my lov - ing　vi - gil keep-ing, All　through the　night.

*Dynamic changes can easily be shown by singing or by playing the song on the piano. It is not as easy for beginning players to do this on the recorder.

Add this part to lines 1, 2, and 4:

Which is the contrasting phrase in this song? When you sing this song, try singing gradually louder, then gradually softer in each phrase. Does this make the music more interesting? Pay particular attention to the dotted-note rhythm whenever it occurs.

New Meter Signatures

JOLLY OLD SAINT NICHOLAS

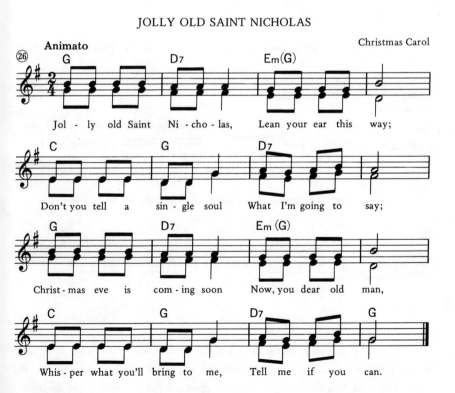

Christmas Carol

Here is the same song again. Is there any difference when you play it this time?

Look at the meter signature of both pieces. One is in $\frac{2}{4}$ meter; the other is in $\frac{2}{2}$.

$\frac{2}{4}$ = two pulses per measure, with the *quarter note* or its equivalent (♩♩ or ♩♫ or ♫♫) getting one pulse.

$\frac{2}{2}$ = *alla breve* or *cut time:* Two pulses per measure, with the *half note* or its equivalent (♩ ♩ or ♫♫ or ♬♬) getting one beat. Many times the sign ¢ is used for $\frac{2}{2}$. These meters are employed to make the notation easier to read.

Let's compare the counting of both, keeping the same pulse.

Remember that & = and.

Divide into two groups and play the song again. This time have one group think in $\frac{2}{4}$ meter while the other thinks in $\frac{2}{2}$ meter. Explain the result.

Play and sing the *Marines' Hymn*, number ㉙ , thinking in $\frac{2}{2}$ meter.

MARINES' HYMN

U. S. Military Song

How many times has the main musical idea been stated?

Here are three meter signatures for *Home on the Range.* Let us compare them.

Look at the $\frac{6}{8}$ example. Notice how many measures there are in comparison with the other two.

In example ㉛, $\frac{3}{8}$ = three beats (pulses) per measure, with the eighth note (♪) or its equivalent (𝅘𝅥𝅮𝅘𝅥𝅮) getting one beat; or one beat per measure, with the dotted quarter note (♩.) or its equivalent (♪♪♪) getting one beat.

In example ㉜, $\frac{6}{8}$ = six beats (pulses) per measure, with the eighth note (♪) or its equivalent (𝅘𝅥𝅮𝅘𝅥𝅮) getting one beat; or two beats per measure, with the dotted quarter note (♩.) or its equivalent (♪♪♪ or ♩ ♪) getting one beat.

What do you see when you compare measures of $\overset{6}{8}$ meter with measures of $\overset{3}{8}$ meter? Divide into three groups, with each group thinking a different meter signature, and play the song together.

HOME ON THE RANGE

In *Home on the Range* how many beats do you feel in each measure?

Feeling the Beat

Stamp the beat, clap, and "ta" the rhythmic patterns, and then play the variations. Create variations of your own.

There are other time syllables possible. You could invent your own.

Variations in $\frac{4}{4}$ meter:

DOWN IN THE VALLEY

Kentucky Folk Song

Down in the val - ley, the val - ley so low,——— Hang your head

o - ver, hear the wind blow,——— Hear the wind

blow, dear, hear the wind blow, ——— Hang your head

o - ver, hear the wind blow.———

2. *Roses love sunshine, violets love dew*
Angels in heaven know I love you.
Know I love you, dear, know I love you,
Angels in heaven know I love you.

3. *Build me a castle forty feet high,*
So I may see him as he rides by.
As he rides by, dear, as he rides by,
So I may see him as he rides by.

How many beats do you feel in each measure of *Down in the Valley?* The meter signature $\frac{9}{8}$ = nine beats per measure, with the eighth note (♪) or its equivalent (♫) getting one beat; or three beats per measure, with the dotted quarter note (♩.) or its equivalent (♪♪♪ or ♩♪ or ♩) getting one beat.

Combining Two Melodies

SANDY LAND

American Singing Game

1. Make my liv - ing in Sand - y Land, Make my liv - ing in

Sand - y Land,   Make my liv -ing in Sand - y Land,

La - dies, fare you well. _____

With recorders, bells, or by singing, add this *descant.*

Sand - y Land,   Sand - y Land

Sand - y Land,   fare you well.

Sandy Land with singing, recorders, Autoharp, and other classroom instruments:

Arr. by Ian H. Johnstone

* ./. means to repeat the previous measure.

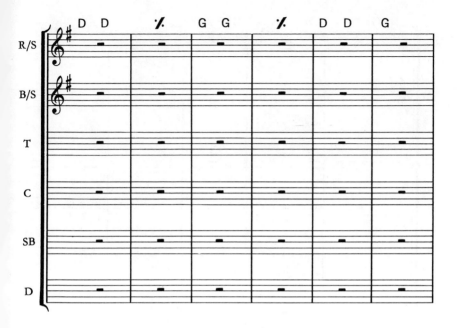

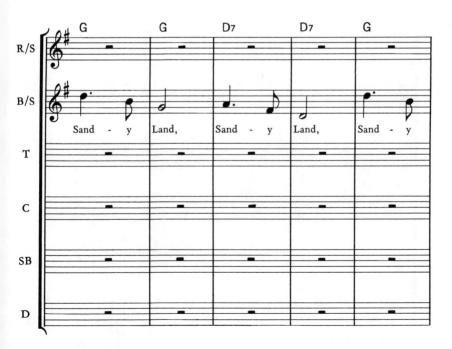

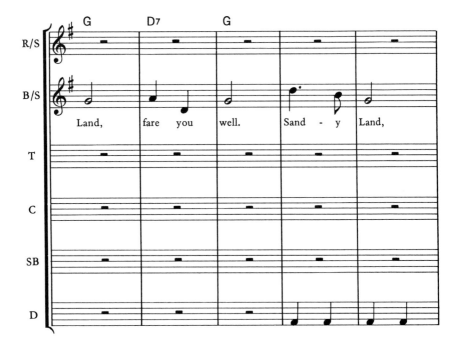

Different instruments add new tone quality (*tone color* or *timbre*) to a composition, and create a new sound. Try performing the song using other tone qualities and different rhythmic patterns.

SHOO, FLY, DON'T BOTHER ME

American Singing Game

Try playing *Shoo, Fly* and *Sandy Land* together. Describe the sound! Melodies that can be played together are often called *quodlibets*, or *partner songs*. They are made possible by having identical harmonization.

Rounds and Canons

BROTHER JOHN
(Frère Jacques)

French Round

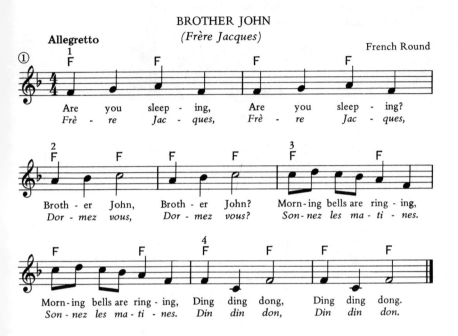

Are you sleep - ing, Are you sleep - ing?
Frè - re Jac - ques, Frè - re Jac - ques,

Broth - er John, Broth - er John? Morn-ing bells are ring - ing,
Dor - mez vous, Dor - mez vous? Son-nez les ma - ti - nes.

Morn-ing bells are ring - ing, Ding ding dong, Ding ding dong.
Son - nez les ma - ti - nes. Din din don, Din din don.

Read the words of *Brother John* to yourself and see if they will help you decide how to use dynamics in this song. Notice that the high pitches of the melody are used with the words "Morning bells are ringing."

You may wish to sing a passage softly *(piano)* and gradually increase the volume of sound to loud *(forte)*. This is called *crescendo*. From forte to piano is called *decrescendo*. Often the signs $\diagup$ and $\diagdown$ are used for crescendo and decrescendo.

Would you rather hear music that is continuously *loud* or continuously *soft* or a combination of the two? Why?

Look at the last measure of *Brother John*. This melodic figure may be used as an ostinato or chant to accompany the song.

Broth - er John Snore Broth - er John

97

Try the song again, adding the ostinato on the melody bells or the piano.

An *ostinato* has been defined as a recurring rhythmic or melodic pattern used as an added part for a song. The term *ostinato* is used when such a pattern is played on an instrument. The term *chant* is used when the pattern is sung. Chants and ostinati add variety to musical experiences.

Other ostinati and chants for this song are:

Chants and ostinati can be used effectively for adding introductions and endings to songs. Try using them in this way.

Sing and play *Brother John* as a two-, three-, or four-part round. What happens to the melody when you sing a song as a round?

Rounds and canons are similar. A round repeats (goes back to the beginning), whereas a canon does not. A round is a circle canon that is in unison; every performer sings the same part, but at different times. Canons may be more complex than rounds, with entrances at different pitch intervals.[1]

LOVELY EVENING

---

[1]Robert Evans Nye and Vernice Trousdale Nye, *Music in The Elementary School*, 4th ed. (Englewood Cliffs, N.J.: Prentice-Hall, 1977), p. 299.

While you stamp the pulse of *Canoe Song,* clap and chant the rhythm of the melody, to help yourself feel the syncopation.

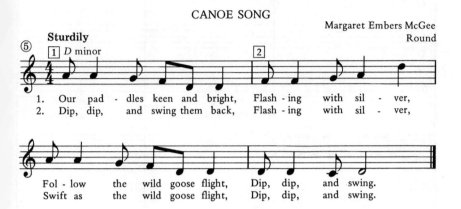

CANOE SONG

Margaret Embers McGee
Round

1. Our pad - dles keen and bright, Flash - ing with sil - ver,
2. Dip, dip, and swing them back, Flash - ing with sil - ver,

Fol - low the wild goose flight, Dip, dip, and swing.
Swift as the wild goose flight, Dip, dip, and swing.

Is this round constructed on a pentatonic scale or on a major scale? On what note do you think this scale is built?

Canoe Song with added tone qualities:

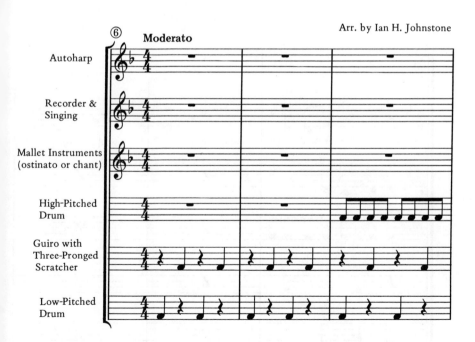

Arr. by Ian H. Johnstone

Dip, dip, and swing, Dip, dip, and swing,

Our pad-dles keen and bright, Flash-ing with sil - ver, Fol-low the wild goose flight,

Flash-ing with sil - ver,   Swift as   the wild goose flight,   Dip, dip,   and swing.

Finger Cymbal

rit.

rit.

Texture

When rounds are performed, the character of the music changes from a one-voiced texture (monophonic) to a many-voiced texture (polyphonic). Texture is that element of music relating to the horizontal and vertical construction of music and the number of parts involved. A single line of melody is of *monophonic* texture. When the melody has a simple chordal accompaniment, a *homophonic* texture is produced. When rounds and canons are performed, the result is a *polyphonic* texture, because two or more parts are sounding at the same time. Some like to think of texture in terms of weaving cloth or fabric, with the lines of melody being similar to the different threads in the weaving process.

CANON IN *G*

German Round

After you know the tune, add the following ostinati:

Is this melody familiar? Play it! See number ⑩.

Playing forward and backwards at the *same* time:

A melody that can be played in canon with the second voice played backwards (in *retrograde*) is called a *cancrizans* or *crab canon* (because crabs walk backwards; cancrizans means "crab").

Play number ⑩ again, adding an Autoharp accompaniment and/or one of the ostinati. The canon has been slightly altered; thus it is not a perfect crab canon.

More Canons to Play and Sing

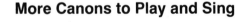

THE DONKEY

Traditional Round

Sweet - ly sings the don - key at the break of day;

If you do not feed him, this is what he'll say, "Hee -

haw,   hee - haw,   hee - haw,   hee - haw   hee - haw! "

The Donkey, with recorders and tone block:

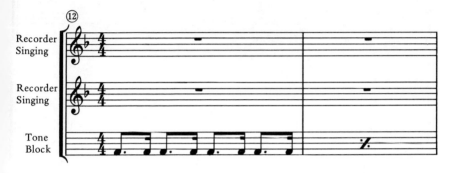

Recorder
Singing

Recorder
Singing

Tone
Block

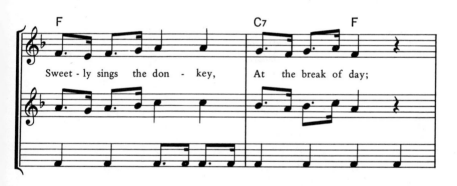

Sweet - ly sings   the don - key,   At   the break of day;

If   you do not feed   him,   This   is what he'll say,   "Hee-

haw,   hee - haw,   hee - haw, hee-haw, hee - haw! "

FOLLOW ON

English Canon

Come a - long,   Sing a - long,   Fol - low

me: It   is   eas - y   as   you   see. Eve - ry

day,   In   this   way,   Just re -

peat,   Till   the   tune's com - plete._____

FOR HEALTH AND STRENGTH

Origin Unknown

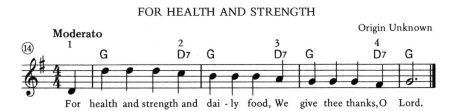

For health and strength and dai - ly food, We give thee thanks, O Lord.

MAN'S LIFE'S A VAPOR

English Round

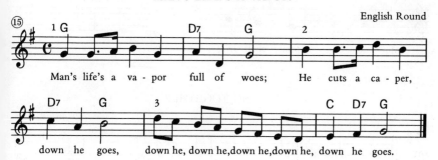

Man's life's a va - por full of woes; He cuts a ca - per, down he goes, down he, down he, down he, down he, down he goes.

GOOD NIGHT TO YOU ALL

Origin Unknown

Good night to you all, and sweet be the sleep; May an - gels a - round you their si - lent watch keep. Good night, good night, good night, good night.

MUSIC ALONE SHALL LIVE

German Round

All things shall per - ish from un - der the sky; Mu - sic a - lone shall live, Mu - sic a - lone shall live,

Mu - sic a - lone shall live, nev - er to die.

SING TOGETHER

Allegro   English Round

(18)

Sing, sing to - geth - er, mer - ri - ly, mer - ri - ly sing:

Sing, sing to - geth - er, mer - ri - ly mer - ri - ly sing;

Sing, sing, sing, sing.

OLD TEXAS

Lento   Cowboy Song

(19)

I'm goin' to leave _____ old Tex - as now, _____ They've got no

use _____ for the long horn cow, _____ They've plowed and

fenced _____ my ___ cat - tle range, _____ and the peo - ple

there _____ are ___ all so strange. _____

DONA NOBIS PACEM
(Give Us Peace)

Origin Unknown

Do - na no - bis pa - cem, pa - cem,

do - na no - bis pa - cem.

Do - na no - bis pa - cem,

do - na no - bis pa - cem,

Do - na no - bis___ pa - cem,

do - na no - bis pa - cem.

UNIT 9

Moving Downward

BROTHER JOHN

French Round

la ti do la   do re mi

mi fa mi re do la   la   so   la

Listen to this melody on a recording of Gustav Mahler's Symphony No. 1, third movement.

Using the melody bells or singing, add the following ostinati and chants.

②

la   so   la   la   so   fa   mi   la   mi   la
Snore, Bro-ther John.   Wake up,   John.   Bro - ther John.

Diatonic Minor Scales

From the key signature used for *Brother John* you might have thought that it was in the key of *F major*, but your ear has already told you that this was not so. *Brother John* is now in the key of *D minor*.

Major scales share their key signatures with minor scales. Minor scales begin on *la (6)* of the major scales. Major and minor keys sharing the same key signature are said to be *relative*. Thus the key signature of one flat (*B♭*) may indicate either an *F major* or a *D minor* tonality.

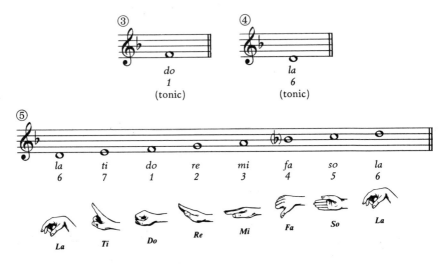

③   ④

do   la
1   6
(tonic)   (tonic)

⑤

la   ti   do   re   mi   fa   so   la
6   7   1   2   3   4   5   6

La   Ti   Do   Re   Mi   Fa   So   La

Sing these scales several times. Play them on the recorder, melody bells, and piano.

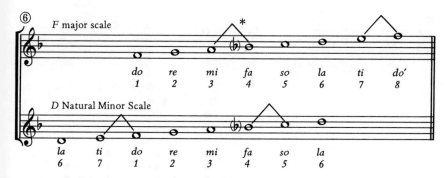

* ∧ indicates where the half steps occur.

The tonal center or tonic for a major scale is *do* or *1*. Since *F* is *do* or *1* in the key of *F* major, *F* is tonic or the tonal center of that key. In a minor key *la (6)* is the tonic or tonal center; therefore, in the key of *D* minor, *D* is *la (6)*.

You can find the relative minor of a major scale by singing or playing down to *la (6)* { do ti la / 1 7 6 }, which then becomes the tonic of the minor scale.

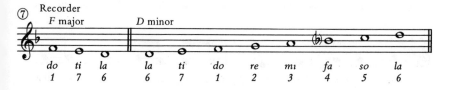

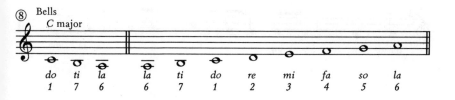

The relative minor of *C* major is _____?

Since the two notes   cannot be played on the soprano recorder, you will have to play the A minor scale an octave higher, using these notes:

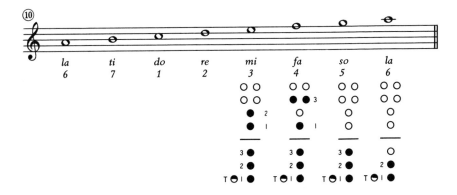

THE BIRCH TREE

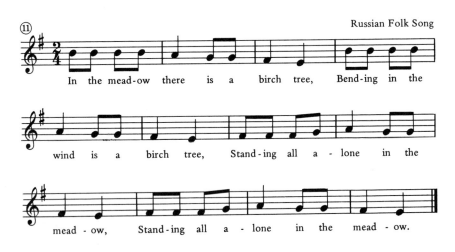

Listen to Tchaikovsky's Symphony No. 4, fourth movement, to hear what a composer does with this melody.

What are the relative keys in this next example? Write the relative minor scale, then play and sing it.

Compare these melodies and chords.

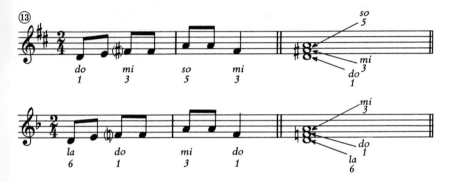

Let us listen to the *D* minor chord played or sung together by three people, or three groups.

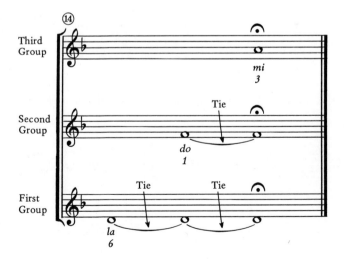

ROUND IN *D* MINOR

Robert E. Nye

la   ti   do   re   mi

so

MELODY IN *D* MINOR

Israeli Folk Tune

la mi   re so re mi

Piano:

Is the complete natural minor scale used in this next melody?

SHALOM, CHAVERIM
(Farewell, Good Friends)

Israeli Round

Fare - well good _ friends, Fare - well Good _ friends, Fare -
well, fare - well! Till we meet a - gain till we
meet a - gain, fare - well, fare - well.

HEY, HO, NOBODY-HOME

Old English Round

Hey, ho, no - bod - y home, Meat and drink and
money have I none, Yet I will be ver - y mer - ry ___
Hey, ho, no - bod - y home.

The following could be used as an introduction or ending *(coda)* to *Hey, Ho, Nobody Home:*

Autoharp

Recorder &
Singing

No - bod - y   home.

Look at the key signature of *Hey, Ho, Nobody Home*. What are the two flats? What is the relative minor of this major scale?

Bb major scale

do re mi fa so la ti do   do ti la
1   2   3   4   5   6   7   8   1   7   6

PICARDY

Traditional French Melody

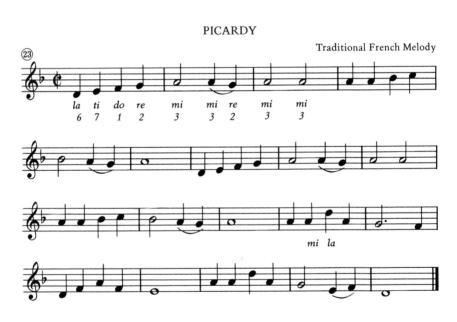

la ti do re   mi   mi re   mi   mi
6   7   1   2   3   3   2   3   3

mi la

A Major–Minor Listening Game

Choose a player to perform the following melodies. After each melody is played, ask the class to decide whether the melody is in a major key or in a minor key.

The Harmonic Minor Scale

GO DOWN, MOSES

Negro Spiritual

When Is - rael was in E - gypt's land, Let my peo - ple go.

Op - pressed so hard they could not stand, Let my peo - ple go.

Go down, Mo - ses, Way down in E - gypt's land,——

Tell ole Pha - raoh, Let my peo - ple go.

Notice that every time the word "people" occurs there is an *F-sharp* (*F* ♯). This *F-sharp* indicates that the melody is based on the *harmonic* minor scale. Let us compare two forms of the G minor scale.

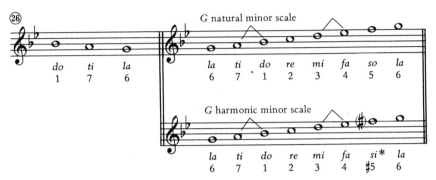

si: pronounced "see."

In the harmonic form of the minor scale the pitch of *so* (5) is raised one half step and is sung to the syllable *si*.

Minor and Major Interspersed

Play and sing *When Johnny Comes Marching Home*. This song uses the natural and harmonic forms of the minor scale. Perform it again and decide which part of the melody uses the natural form, and which part uses the harmonic form.

WHEN JOHNNY COMES MARCHING HOME

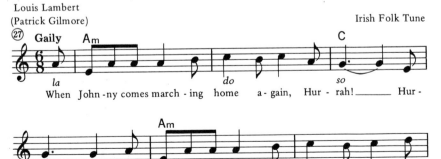

C	E7	Am

mi!   *do*   *mi*
- rah!_____   Hur - rah!_____   The___ men   will cheer,___ the

E7	Am	E7

re   *do*   *ti*
boys will shout, The   la - dies,they___ will   all   turn   out, And we'll

Am	Dm	Am	E7	Am

mi   *re*   *do*   *ti*   *la*   *si*   *la*
all   feel   glad   when   John-ny comes march-ing home._____

Sometimes relative major and minor keys are used in the same song. Such is the case with *We Three Kings of Orient Are* and *The Erie Canal*. Decide which section of each song is in a minor key, and which sections use the relative major. *Remember* that relative keys have the same key signature.

WE THREE KINGS OF ORIENT ARE

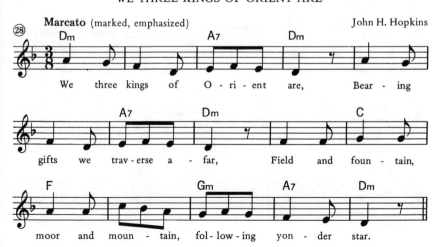

Marcato (marked, emphasized)   John H. Hopkins

Dm	A7	Dm

We   three   kings   of   O - ri - ent   are,   Bear - ing

A7	Dm	C

gifts   we   trav - erse   a - far,   Field   and   foun - tain,

F	Gm	A7	Dm

moor   and   moun - tain,   fol - low - ing   yon - der   star.

Refrain

Oh, _____ star of won - der, star of night,

star with roy - al beau - ty bright,

West - ward lead - ing, still pro - ceed - ing,

guide us to the per - fect light.

ERIE CANAL

American Folk Song

29 **Robustly**

1. I've got a mule, her name is Sal, Fif - teen miles on the

E - rie Ca - nal. She's a good old work - er and a

good old pal, Fif - teen miles on the E - rie Ca - nal. We've

hauled some barg - es in our day, Filled with lum - ber,

coal and hay, And we know eve - ry inch of the way, From

Al - ba - ny ____ to ____ Buf - fa - lo. ____

Chorus

Low bridge, eve - ry - bod - y down,

Low bridge, 'cause were com - ing to a town; And you'll

al - ways know your neigh - bor, you'll al - ways know your pal, If you've

ev - er nav - i - gat - ed on the E - rie Ca - nal.

*B♮ in the key of F major is called *fi* or ♯4. *Fi* is pronounced "fee."

Modes

   Through Hebrew, Greek, Roman, and medieval European history, there have evolved six scales that are called "the modes," *mode* being another name for scale. Two of these modes, the Ionian and the Aeolian, are the major and minor scales of today. The other four modes—Dorian, Phrygian, Lydian, and Mixolydian—are both archaic and contemporary, being found in folk music and in some music written today. Some spirituals and blues are based on the Mixolydian mode.

The world of music possesses many scales, but those in most common use are the pentatonic scales described in this book, the major and minor scales, and the four less common modes. Songs that are based on one of those four scales include *Carol Canon, Greensleeves, Scarborough Fair,* and *Every Night When the Sun Goes In,* all in Unit 10.

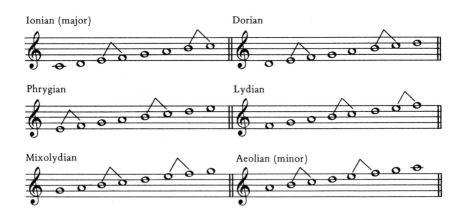

UNIT 10

More Music to Sing and Play

SLEEPERS, WAKE! A VOICE IS CALLING

Tune by Philipp Nicolai
Harmonized by Johann Sebastian Bach

Related listening: Cantata No. 140, by Johann Sebastian Bach.

HANUKKAH

Jewish Song

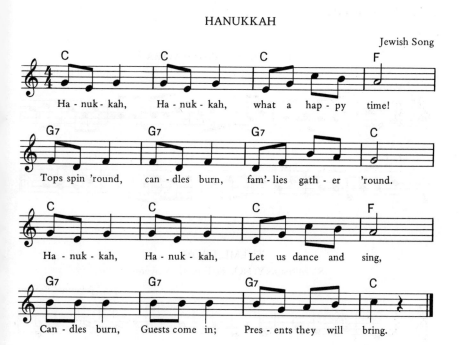

Ha - nuk - kah,   Ha - nuk - kah,   what a   hap - py   time!

Tops spin 'round,   can - dles burn,   fam'- lies   gath - er   'round.

Ha - nuk - kah,   Ha - nuk - kah,   Let   us   dance   and   sing,

Can - dles   burn,   Guests come in;   Pres - ents they   will   bring.

HYMN FROM *FINLANDIA*

Related listening: *Finlandia,* tone poem by Jan Sibelius.

THE IRISH WASHERWOMAN

THEME FROM
SYMPHONY NO. 1, Fourth Movement

Related listening: Symphony No. 1, fourth movement, by Johannes Brahms.

EMPEROR'S HYMN
(Austria)

John Newton

Franz Joseph Haydn

March tempo

Glo-rious things of thee are spo - ken, Zi - on, cit - y of our— God;

He, whose word can - not be bro - ken, Formed thee for his

own a - bode; On the Rock—of A - ges foun - ded,

what can shake thy sure re- pose? With sal - va - tion's

wall sur - round - ed, Thou may'st smile— at— all thy— foes.

Related listening: Quartet in C Major ("The Emperor"), second movement, by Franz Joseph Haydn.

CAROL CANON

Allegretto   Traditional French Canon

STREETS OF LAREDO

Canon for three recorders

Cowboy Song

1. As I_____ walked out in the streets of La - re - do,
2. "I see by your out - fit that you are a cow - boy,"

As I_____ walked out in La - re - do one day
These words he did say as I bold - ly walked by;

I spied a young cow - boy all wrapped in white lin - en,_____
"Come set down be - side me and hear my sad stor - y, I'm

Wrapped in white lin - en as cold as the clay.
Shot in the breast and I know I must die."

3. "It was once in the saddle I used to go dashing,
Once in the saddle I used to go gay;
First down to Rosie's and then to the card-house;
Got shot in the breast and I'm dyin' today.

4. "Get sixteen gamblers to handle my coffin,
Let six jolly cowboys come sing me a song,
Take me to the graveyard and lay the sod o'er me,
For I'm a young cowboy, I know I've done wrong.

5. "Oh, beat the drum slowly and play the fife lowly,
Play the dead march as they carry me along,
Put bunches of roses all over my coffin,
Roses to deaden the clods as they fall."

6. (Repeat Verse 1.)

EVERY NIGHT WHEN THE SUN GOES IN

American Folk Song

Andante

Ev'- ry night ———— when the sun goes in, ————
Ev'- ry night ———— when the sun goes in, ————
Ev'- ry night ———— when the sun goes in, ————
I hang down my head ———— and mourn-ful cry. ————

CINDY

American Folk Song

Vivace

You ought to see my Cin - dy, She lives a - way down south,
And she's so sweet the hon - ey bees,— Swarm a - round her mouth.

Git a-long home, Cin - dy, Cin - dy, Git a-long home, Cin - dy, Cin - dy,

Git a-long home, Cin - dy, Cin - dy, I'll mar - ry you some - time.

AMAZING GRACE

John Newton

Traditional American Melody
Arr. by Robert E. Nye

A - maz - ing grace! how sweet the sound,

That saved a child like me!

I once was lost, but now am found,

Was blind but now I see.

2. 'Twas grace that taught my heart to
   fear,
And grace my fears relieved;
How precious did that grace appear
The hour I first believed!

3. The Lord has promised good to me,
His word my hope secures;
He will my shield and portion be
As long as life endures.

SILENT NIGHT

Franz Gruber   Joseph Mohr

1. Si - lent night, ho - ly night, All is calm,
2. Si - lent night, ho - ly night, Shep - herds quake

all is bright, Round yon Vir - gin Moth - er and Child,
at the sight, Glo - ries stream — from heav - en a - far,

Ho - ly in - fant so ten - der and mild, Sleep in heav - en - ly
Heav'n - ly hosts — sing "Al - le - lu - ia; Christ, the Sav - ior is

peace, ___ Sleep ___ in heav - en - ly peace. ___
born, ___ Christ ___ the Sav - ior is born! " ___

THE HURON CAROL

Dr. J. E. Middleton   Jesuit Song from Canada

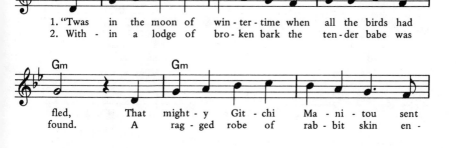

1. "Twas in the moon of win - ter - time when all the birds had
2. With - in a lodge of bro - ken bark the ten - der babe was

fled, That might - y Git - chi Ma - ni - tou sent
found. A rag - ged robe of rab - bit skin en -

an - gel   choirs   in - stead.   Be - fore their light the
wrapp'd his beau - ty   'round.   And   as   the   hun - ter

stars grew dim   and   wan - d'ring hun - ters   heard the   hymn:___
braves drew nigh the   an - gel   song   rang   loud and   high:___

Refrain

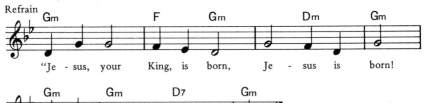

"Je - sus,   your   King,   is   born,   Je - sus   is   born!

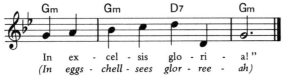

In   ex - cel - sis   glo - ri - a!"
(In   eggs - chell - sees   glor - ree - ah)

3. *The earliest moon of wintertime is not*
   so round and fair
As was the ring of glory on the helpless
   Infant there.
The chiefs from far, before Him knelt
   with gifts of fox and beaver pelt.
Refrain

PAT-A-PAN

Burgundian Carol
Translated by H. Virginia Nye   Arr. by Robert E. Nye

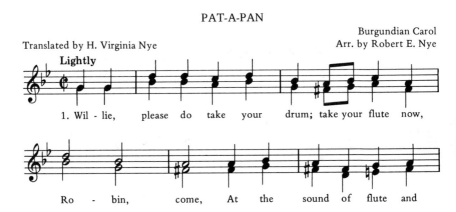

Lightly

1. Wil - lie,   please   do   take   your   drum; take your flute   now,

Ro - bin,   come,   At   the   sound   of   flute   and

drum,   Tu - re - lu - re - lu,   pat - a - pat - a - pan,   At   the

sound   of   flute   and   drum, we'll be mer - ry,   ev - 'ry - one!

2. *When the men of old did sing praises*
   to the King of Kings,
At the sound of flute and drum, Tu-re-
lu-re-lu, pat-a-pat-a-pan,
At the sound of flute and drum they were
merry, ev'ryone!

3. *God and man are now in tune, like the*
   ringing flute and drum,
At the sound of flute and drum, Tu-re-
lu-re-lu, pat-a-pat-a-pan,
At the sound of flute and drum, sing and
dance now, ev'ryone!

Reprinted by permission from *Toward World Understanding With Song.* Copyright 1967 by Vernice T. Nye, Robert E. Nye, and H. Virginia Nye.

Improvise an accompaniment on the Autoharp by holding down both G major and G minor bars throughout and making up your own strumming.

NOCTURNE
Duet

Robert E. Nye

* See next page for G♯ fingering.

THEME FROM *CAPRICCIO ITALIAN*

Peter Ilich Tschaikovsky

Tempo di Valse

*Alternate fingering. Here are the two fingerings for G♯ /A♭:

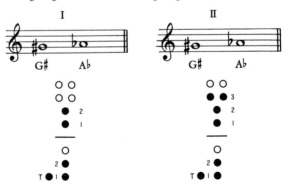

Related listening: *Capriccio Italien,* by Peter Ilich Tchaikovsky.

ANGELS WE HAVE HEARD ON HIGH

With joy   Traditional French Carol

1. An-gels we have heard on high, Sweet-ly sing-ing o'er the plains,

And the moun-tains in re-ply, Ech-o-ing their joy-ous strains.

Chorus

Glo - - - - - - - - - - - - - -

- -ri - a in ex - cel - sis De - o,

Glo - - - - - - - - - - - - - -

- ri - a in ex - cel - sis De - - o.

2. *Shepherds, why this jubilee?*
Why your joyous strains prolong?
What the gladsome tidings be
Which inspire your heavenly song?

3. *Come to Bethlehem and see*
Him whose birth the angels sing;
Come, adore on bended knee
Christ, the Lord, the newborn King.

WAYFARING STRANGER

American Folk Song
Arr. by Robert E. Nye

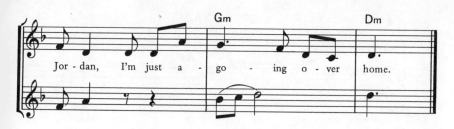

Jor - dan,   I'm just a - go -   ing   o - ver   home.

GREENSLEEVES

Moderately   Old English Melody

A - las!   my love, ___ you   do   me   wrong, ___ To
cast   me off ___ dis - cour - teous - ly;   And   I   have lov - ed
you   so long, ___ De - light - ing in ___ your   com - pa - ny.
Refrain
Green - - sleeves ___ was   all   my   joy. ___
Green - sleeves ___ was   my   de - light,   Green - sleeves, ___ my
heart   of gold, ___ And   all   but my La -   dy   Green - sleeves.

Related listening: *Fantasia on Greensleeves,* by Ralph Vaughan Williams.

SCARBOROUGH FAIR

English Ballad

1. Are   you   go - ing   to   Scar - bor - ough   fair,
2. Tell   her   to   make   me   a   cam - bric   shirt,
3. Tell   her   to   wash   it   in   yon - der   well,

Re - mem - ber   me___   to
Pars - ley, sage, rose - ma - ry, and thyme; With - out   any seam___ or
Where   never spring wa - ter nor

JOHNNY HAS GONE FOR A SOLDIER

Traditional Irish Melody
Arr. by Robert E. Nye

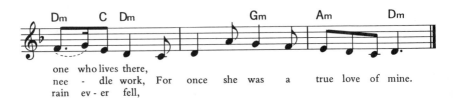

one who lives there,
nee - dle work,   For   once   she   was   a   true   love   of   mine.
rain   ev - er   fell,

JESU, JOY OF MAN'S DESIRING

Johann Schop
Arr. by Johann Sebastian Bach,
Robert E. Nye

*See Appendix A for fingering.

Related listening: Cantata No. 147, by Johann Sebastian Bach.

O SACRED HEAD, NOW WOUNDED

Harmonized by Johann Sebastian Bach

*See Appendix A for fingering.

Related listening: St. Matthew Passion, by Johann Sebastian Bach.

THEME FROM
PIANO SONATA K. 331, first movement

Wolfgang Amadeus Mozart
Arr. by Robert E. Nye

Staccato: perform in a disconnected manner.

Related listening: Piano Sonata K. 331, first movement, by Wolfgang Amadeus Mozart.

ST. ANTHONY CHORALE

Franz Joseph Haydn

Related listening: *Variations on a Theme by Haydn,* by Johannes Brahms.

THE CANADIAN

Yvonne Carr   French Canadian Folk Tune

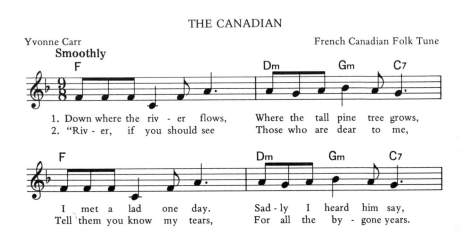

1. Down where the riv - er flows, Where the tall pine tree grows,
2. "Riv - er, if you should see Those who are dear to me,

I met a lad one day. Sad - ly I heard him say,
Tell them you know my tears, For all the by - gone years.

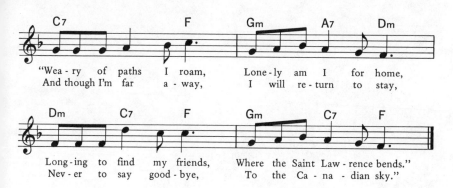

"Wea - ry of paths I roam, Lone-ly am I for home,
And though I'm far a - way, I will re - turn to stay,

Long - ing to find my friends, Where the Saint Law - rence bends."
Nev - er to say good - bye, To the Ca - na - dian sky."

Reprinted from H. R. Wilson *et al., Growing With Music,* Book 5 (Englewood Cliffs, N.J.: Prentice-Hall, Inc., 1966), p. 24, by permission of the publisher.

O COME, O COME, EMMANUEL

Plain Song
Words Translated by John M. Neale

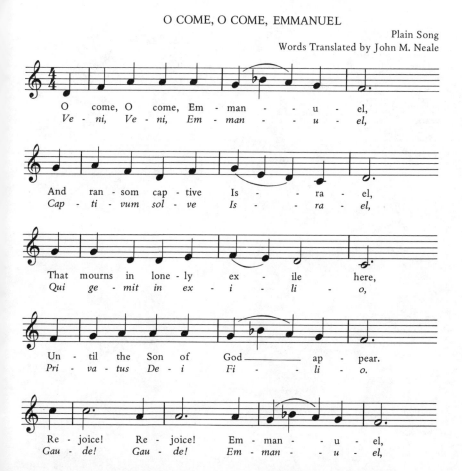

O come, O come, Em - man - u - el,
Ve - ni, Ve - ni, Em - man - u - el,

And ran - som cap - tive Is - ra - el,
Cap - ti - vum sol - ve Is - ra - el,

That mourns in lone - ly ex - ile here,
Qui ge - mit in ex - i - li - o,

Un - til the Son of God ap - pear.
Pri - va - tus De - i Fi - li - o.

Re - joice! Re - joice! Em - man - u - el,
Gau - de! Gau - de! Em - man - u - el,

Shall   come   to   thee,   O   Is   -   - ra   - el.
Nas - ce - tur   pro   te,   Is   -   - ra   - el.

COVENTRY CAROL

English Carol

Tenderly

1. Lul - lay, Thou   lit - tle   ti - ny   Child,   By, by, lul -
2. O   sis - ters, too, how   may   we   do,   For to pre -

ly   lul - lay;_____   Lul - lay, Thou   lit - tle
serve   this   day;_____   This   poor,   Young - ling   for

ti - ny   Child,   By, by, lul - ly, lul - lay._____
whom   we   sing?   By, by, lul - ly, lul - lay._____

REFERENCES

Autoharp

NYE, ROBERT E., and MEG PETERSON, *Teaching Music With the Autoharp.* Union, N.J. 07083: Music Education Group, 1973.

Guitar

EISENKRAMER, HENRY E., *Strum and Sing: Guitar in the Classroom.* Evanston, Ill.: Summy-Birchard Co., 1969.

Guitar Magic. Atlanta, Ga.: Educational Productions, Inc., 454 Armour Circle. N.E. 30324. An audiovisual method.

Mel Bay's Guitar Class Method. Kirkwood, Mo.: Mel Bay Publications, Inc., 107 W. Jefferson Ave. 63122.

SILVERMAN, JERRY, *Graded Guitar Method.* New York: The Big Three Music Corp., 1970.

TIMMERMAN, MAURINE, and CELESTE GRIFFITH, *Guitar in the Classroom.* Dubuque, Iowa: William C. Brown Company, Publishers, 1971.

Multiple Instruments

BURAKOFF, GERALD, and LAWRENCE WHEELER, *Music Making in the Elementary School.* New York, N.Y. 10018: Hargail Music, Inc. Student's and Teacher's Editions. Uses recorder, voice, bells, and rhythm instruments.

CHEYETTE, IRVING, and ALBERT RENNA, *Songs to Sing with Recreational Instruments.* Philadelphia, Pa.: Theodore Presser Company.

SNYDER, ALICE M., *Sing and Strum.* Melville, N.Y. 11746: Belwin-Mills.

VANDRE, CARL, *Adventures in Harmony, Rhythm, and Song.* Minneapolis, Minn.: Handy-Folio Music Company.

WIEDINMEYER, CLEMENT, *Play-Sing-Chord Along.* Delaware Water Gap, Pa.: Shawnee Press.

Piano Chording

Easy:
ECKSTEIN, MAXWELL, *Play It Now.* New York, N.Y.: Carl Fisher.

FRISCH, FAY TEMPLETON, *The Play-Way to Music, Book Two.* New York, N.Y.: Amsco Music Publications, Inc.

NEVIN, MARK, *Tunes You Like,* Books 1, 2, 3, 4. New York, N.Y.: Schroeder and Gunther, Inc.

NEVIN, MARK, *Repertoire Album,* Book I. Melville, N.Y.: Belwin, Inc.

STEINER, ERIC, *One, Four, Five.* Mills Music, Inc.: *Repertoire Album Book I,* Melville, N.Y.: Belwin, Inc.

Slightly more difficult:
BERMONT, GEORGES, *Play That Tune,* Books 1, 2, 3, 4. Staten Island, N.Y.: Musicord Publications.

115 Easy Piano Pieces and Folk Songs. Moonachie, N.J.: Hansen Publications.

RICHTER, ADA, *Songs I Can Play.* New York, N.Y.: M. Witmark and Sons.

STICKLES, WILLIAM, *Easy Hymns and Sacred Songs for the Piano.* Moonachie, N.J.: Hansen Publications.

Recorder

Literature
BURAKOFF, GERALD, *The School Recorder, Background Material and Guidelines For Teachers.* Hicksville, N.Y.: Consort Music, 1973.

BURAKOFF, GERALD, *The Recorder in the Classroom.* New York: Hargail Music Press, 1971.

The American Recorder. The magazine of the American Recorder Society, published quarterly. The American Recorder Society, Inc., 141 West 20th St., New York, N.Y. 10011.

Recorder and Music. The magazine of The Society of Recorder Players of Great Britain, published quarterly. Schott and Co. Ltd., 48 Great Marlborough St., London, England, WIV 2 BN. Also Magnamusic Distributors, Inc., Sharon, Conn., 06069.

Supplementary Material

BERGMAN, WALTER, *Sixteen American Folksongs*. New York: Hargail Music Press, 1973.

BURAKOFF, GERALD, and SONYA BURAKOFF, *The Classroom Recorder*, Book 2. Hicksville, N.Y.: Consort Music, 1970.

BURAKOFF, GERALD, and WILLY STRICKLAND, *The Duet Recorder*, Books 1 and 2. Hicksville, N.Y.: Consort Music, 1970, 1972.

BURAKOFF, GERALD, and WILLY STRICKLAND, *First Performance*. Hicksville, N.Y.: Consort Music.

BURAKOFF, GERALD, and WILLY STRICKLAND, *The Holiday Recorder*. Hicksville, N.Y.: Consort Music, 1970.

BURAKOFF, GERALD, and LAWRENCE WHEELER, *Music Making in the Elementary School*. New York: Hargail Music Press, 1968.

COLES, GRAHAM, *Folksongs of Canada*. Toronto: Berandel Music Ltd., 1976.

KULBACK, JOHANNA, *Tunes For Children*. Browns Mills, N.J.: Carl Van Roy Company, 1959.

NEWMAN, HAROLD, and MIECYSLAW KOLINSKI, *The Children's Song Book*. New York: Hargail Music Press, 1967.

NITKA, ARTHUR, *One-Two-Three-Play!* Brooklyn, N.Y.: Anfer Music Publishing, 1962.

ROTHGARBER, HERBERT, *Make a Glad Sound*. Hicksville, N.Y.: Consort Music.

TAYLOR, MARY C., *Rounds and Rounds We Go*. Brooklyn, N.Y.: Anfer Music Publishing, 1969.

TRAPP FAMILY SINGERS, *Enjoying Your Recorder*. Sharon, Conn.: Magnamusic Distributors, Inc., 1954.

WHEELER, LAWRENCE, *The Ensemble Recorder*, Hicksville, N.Y.: Consort Music, 1970.

WHITNEY, MAURICE C., *Folk Songs of America*. Hicksville, N.Y.: Consort Music, 1970.

WHITNEY, MAURICE C., *Folk Songs of Europe*. Hicksville, N.Y.: Consort Music.

WHITNEY, MAURICE C., *Eleven Traditional Hymns*. Hicksville, N.Y.: Consort Music, 1972.

Suppliers of Recorders and/or Recorder Materials

Anfor Music Publishers, 17 West 60th St., New York, N.Y. 10023.

Associated Music Publishers, Inc., 609 Fifth Ave., New York, N.Y. 10017. Distributor for B.M.I. and Deblinger.

Belwin Mills Publishing Corp., Rockville Centre, N.Y. 11571. Distributor for Schott.

Consort Music Inc., P.O. Box 371, Hicksville, N.Y. 11802

E. C. Schirmer Music Co., 600 Washington St., Boston, Mass. 02111

Galaxy Music Corp., 2121 Broadway, N.Y. 10023. Distributor for American Recorder Society editions.

Hargail Music Press, 28 West 38th St., New York, N.Y. 10018. Distributor for Barenreiter, Hofmeister, XYZ, Academia, Melodie, and other European publishers. Music of all publishers available.

Magnamusic Distributors, Inc., Sharon, Conn. 06069, and/or Magnamusic-Baton, Inc., 10370 Page Industrial Blvd., St. Louis, Mo. 63132.

Oxford University Press, 200 Madison Ave., New York, N.Y. 10016.

C. F. Peters Corp., 373 Park Avenue South, New York, N.Y. 10016. Distributor for Hinrichsen, Neetzel, and other European publishers.

Recorder Shop, The, 309 W. Fourth St., Los Angeles, Calif. 90013.

Theodore Presser Co., Bryn Mawr, Pa. 19010. Distributor for Universal Edition.

Trophy Music Company, 1278 W. 9th St., Cleveland, Ohio 44113.

There are a great many sources of recorders. Examples of low-priced instruments are the Aulos Recorder (Music Sales Corporation, 33 West 60th Street, New York, N.Y. 10023), claimed to be "dishwasher safe" for sterilization, and the Harvard Recorder (Hargail Music, Inc. 28 West 38th Street, New York, N.Y. 10018), a three-piece instrument. School districts often obtain school discounts from suppliers of recorders.

APPENDIXES

APPENDIX A   Soprano Recorder Fingering Chart (English or Baroque Fingering)

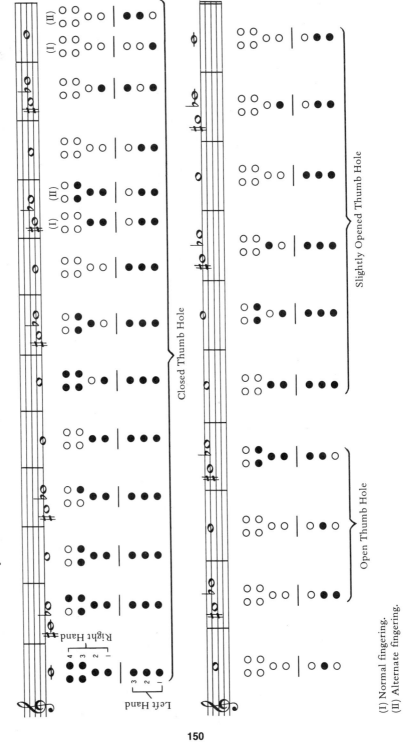

(I) Normal fingering.
(II) Alternate fingering.

Ukulele and Guitar Fingering Chart

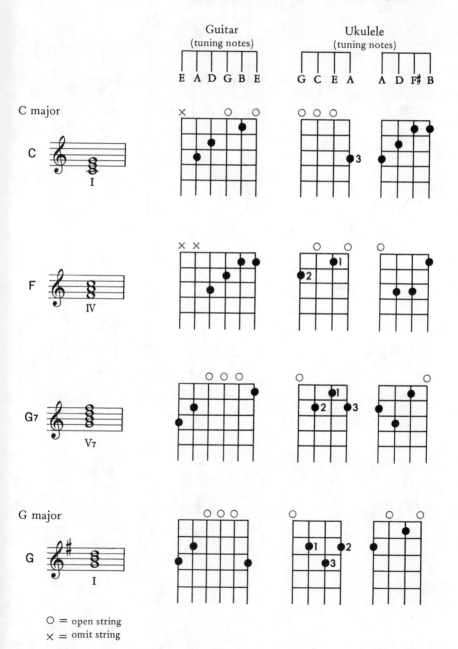

O = open string
× = omit string

152

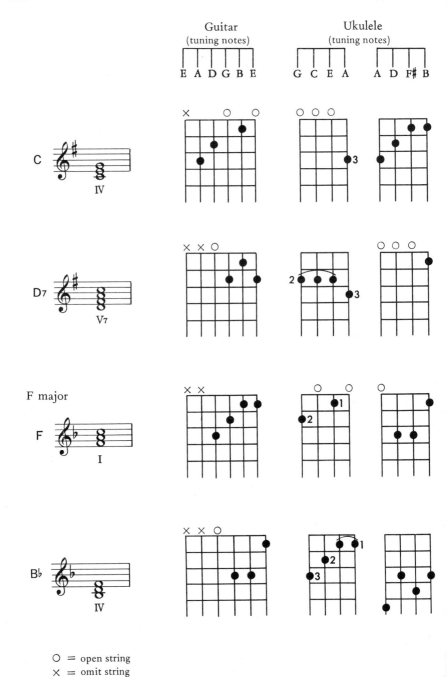

Appendix B

Guitar (tuning notes)

Ukulele (tuning notes)

E A D G B E

G C E A

A D F♯ B

C

IV

D7

V7

F major

F

I

B♭

IV

○ = open string
✕ = omit string

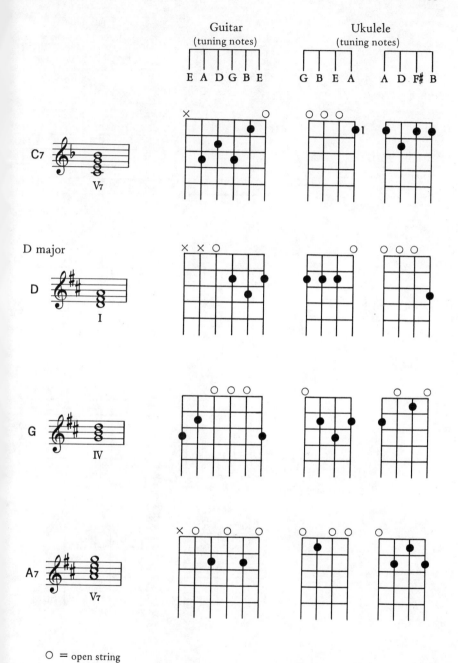

○ = open string

× = omit string

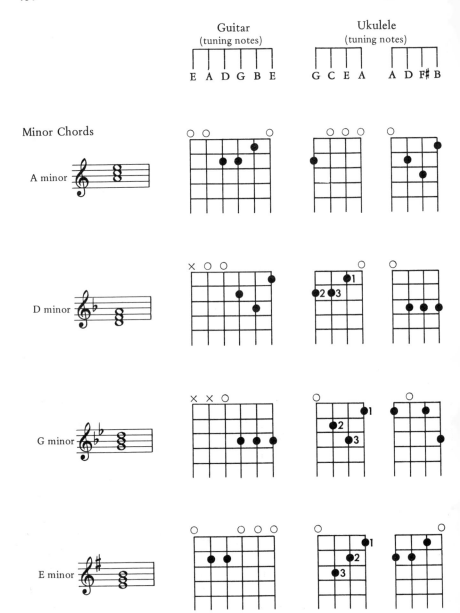

Minor Chords

A minor

D minor

G minor

E minor

○ = open string
× = omit string

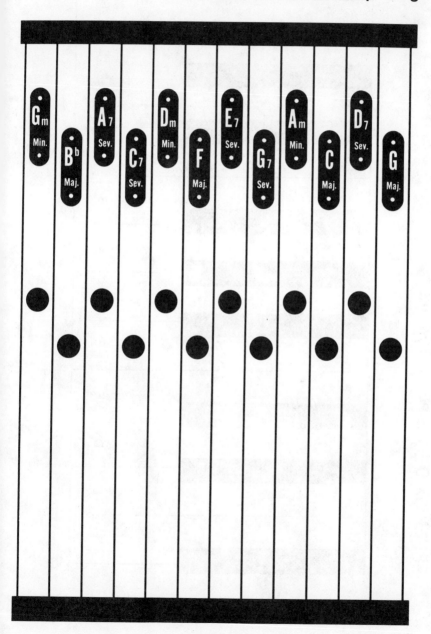

APPENDIX D   The Piano Keyboard

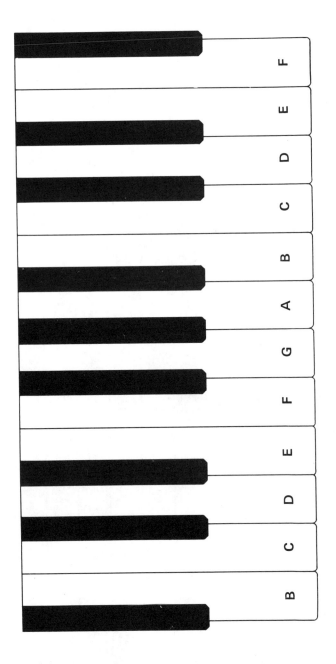

Finding the Keynote in Major Tonalities

This is necessary to enable the student to establish the pitch and key feeling of a song. The ways to find the keynote from key signatures are:

1. The sharp farthest to the right is scale tone *7* or *ti*. Count up to *8* or *do*. The letter name of *8 (1)* or *do* is the name of the key.

2. The flat farthest to the right is scale tone *4* or *fa*. Count down to *1* or up to *8;* the letter name of *8* or *1* is the name of the key. A quicker way for key signatures containing two or more flats is: the next-to-the-last flat on the right *is* the keynote.

Songs in major tonalities ordinarily end on *1, 3,* or *5 (do, mi,* or *so).*

Finding the Keynote in Minor Tonalities

1. Find the major tonality indicated by the key signature

2. Find the sixth degree of the major scale *(6* or *la).* This note is the keynote of the relative minor tonality

Songs in minor usually end on *la,* rarely on *do* or *mi.*

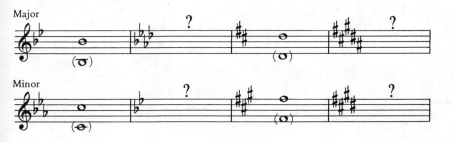

APPENDIX F
Suppliers of Classroom Instruments

CHILDREN'S MUSIC CENTER, 5373 West Pico Blvd., Los Angeles, Calif. 90019.

CONTINENTAL MUSIC, Division of C. G. Conn, Ltd., 150 Aldredge Blvd., Atlanta, Ga. 30336.

B. F. KITCHING, 505 Shawmut St., LaGrange, Ill. 60525

LYONS, 530 Riverview Ave., Elkhart, Ind. 46514.

MAGNAMUSIC-BATON, INC., 10370 Page Industrial Blvd., St. Louis, Mo. 63132.

MUSIC EDUCATION GROUP, Garden State Road, Union, N.J. 07083. Autoharp and all other instruments.

RHYTHM BAND, INC., P.O. Box 126, Fort Worth, Texas 76101.

SCIENTIFIC INDUSTRIES, INC., 823 S. Wabash Ave., Chicago 60605. Song Bells and Tone Educator Bells.

WEXLER, 823 S. Wabash Ave., Chicago 60605.

WORLD OF PERIPOLE, INC., P.O. Box 146, Lewiston Road, Browns Mills, N.J. 08015.

APPENDIX G
Common Musical Terms

TERM	*MEANING*
Accelerando (accel.)	Gradually increasing the speed
Adagio	Slowly, leisurely
Allegretto	Moderately fast, slower than allegro
Allegro	Lively, brisk, rapid
Andante	Moderately slow
Animato	With animation
A tempo	In the original tempo
Con	With
Con moto	With motion
Con spirito	With spirit
Coda	A supplement at end of composition
Crescendo (cresc.)	Increasing in loudness
Da Capo (D.C.)	From the beginning
Dal Segno (D.S.)	From the sign
Decrescendo (decresc.)	Decreasing in loudness
Diminuendo (dim.)	Gradually softer
Dolce (dol.)	Softly, sweetly
Espressivo	With expression
Fermata	Hold (prolong)
Fine	The end
Forte (f)	Loud
Forte-piano (fp)	Accent strongly, diminishing
Fortissimo (ff)	Very loud
Grandioso	Grand, pompous, majestic
Grave	Very slow
Largo	Broad and slow
Legato	Smoothly, the reverse of staccato
Lento	Slow, between andante and largo
Maestoso	Majestically, dignified
Mezzo piano (mp)	Moderately soft
Moderato	Moderately

TERM	MEANING
Pianissimo (pp)	Very softly
Piano (p)	Softly
Presto	Very quick
Rallentando (rall.)	Gradually slower
Ritardando (rit.)	Gradually slower and slower
Ritenuto	In slower time
Sforzando (sf)	Forcibly, with sudden emphasis
Sostenuto	sustained, prolonged
Staccato	Detached, separate
Tempo	Movement, rate of speed
Tranquillo	Quietly
Troppo	Much
Un poco	A little
Vivace	Bright, spirited
Vivo	Lively, spirited

INDEXES

Triplet, 41

Ukulele, 151
Unity, 29
Up-beat, 78–80

Variations, 87
Variety, 29

Whole-step, 58

Index of Songs and Instrumental Titles